HEALTH REPORTS:
DISEASES AND DISORDERS

AUTISM SPECTRUM DISORDERS

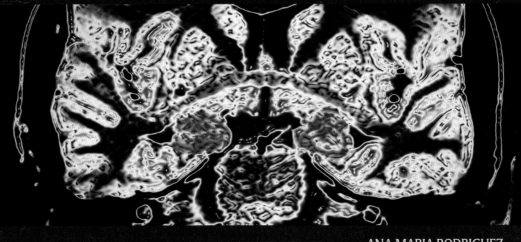

ANA MARIA RODRIGUEZ

TWENTY-FIRST CENTURY BOOKS
MINNEAPOLIS

To my husband and sons, with love

Twenty-First Century Books
A division of Lerner Publishing Group, Inc.
241 First Avenue North
Minneapolis, MN 55401 U.S.A.

Website address: www.lernerbooks.com

Library of Congress Cataloging-in-Publication Data

Rodriguez, Ana Maria, 1958–
       Autism spectrum disorders / by Ana Maria Rodriguez.
              p. cm. — (USA today health reports. Diseases and disorders)
       Includes bibliographical references and index.
       ISBN 978-0-7613-5883-1 (lib. bdg. : alk. paper)
       1. Autism spectrum disorders—Juvenile literature. I. Title.
    RC553.A88R636 2011
    616.85'88—dc22   2010034236

Manufactured in the United States of America
1 – DP – 12/31/10

CONTENTS

USA TODAY
HEALTH REPORTS:
DISEASES AND DISORDERS

CHAPTER ONE

A DIFFERENT KIND OF MIND

PETER'S STORY

When he was a baby, Peter was the complete opposite of his older sister, Julie. She had been extremely active and talkative. Peter, on the other hand, was quiet and detached. But his parents, Dan and Juliet, had heard many times that siblings can be very different from one another. And they had heard that boys tended to develop later than girls. So at first, they didn't worry about Peter's behavior.

Peter was quite independent. He preferred to be on his own instead of playing games with his parents. He never cried when his parents left the room. Dan and Juliet worked from home, and Peter would lie silently on his back on the floor staring at the ceiling while they sat at their desks. As Peter grew, he would entertain himself for hours by touching his fingers together and flicking them. Or he pulled off the fringe of the area rug and rubbed the material between his fingers. In the summer, Peter would sit in a little inflatable swimming pool in the backyard and splash for the whole afternoon.

Peter had sensitive hearing. Some noises would upset him, such as the roar of a motorcycle or the doorbell ringing. When he heard these sounds, he would cover his ears and rock back and forth. Sometimes, he would hit his head with both fists. And while most babies begin speaking when they are about one year old, Peter was still not speaking at fifteen months.

As a toddler, Peter enjoyed going to the local playground with Juliet. As soon as they arrived, Peter began what the family called his "bird routine." He energetically flapped his hands and spun around, eyes wide open, face tilted toward the sky. He never seemed to get dizzy. He would spin around and around and stop and flick his fingers as if trying to remove dirt. Then he would begin his bird routine again.

If other children tried to join him, Peter ignored them. Juliet assumed Peter did not pay attention to the children because he was so focused on his own activity. Soon the other kids began to leave him alone.

One day when Peter was about nineteen months old, he and Juliet were leaving the playground. Another mother approached them. She handed Juliet a note and smiled. Peter was pulling at his mother's hand, impatient to leave, so she did not have a chance to talk to the other mother. But once in the car, Juliet opened the note. It read, "Look up PDD."

Juliet did not know what this meant. Thinking it must be some kind of code, she went home and looked up PDD on the Internet. What she found caught her off guard. PDD stands for "pervasive developmental disorder." It refers to a group of disorders that affect a child's development in areas such as speech and social skills. When she read the definition, she recognized her own son.

Peter's parents quickly took him to a pediatric neurologist, a doctor who specializes in children's brain disorders. They then took him to a developmental pediatrician, a doctor trained to assess childhood development patterns. When tested, Peter showed significantly low scores in intelligence, communication skills, social skills, and everyday behavior. Peter was diagnosed with a PDD called autism.

JEFF'S STORY

When Jeff was two years old, he spent hours lining up toy cars and gazing at them from different angles. He did not turn when his name was called or take any notice of other people around him. Once when his mother hurt herself and cried out in pain, Jeff did not respond.

When he first began speaking, he did not use words to communicate. Instead, he would echo back phrases from the television news. He also watched the credits at the end of TV shows and arranged plastic letters to form the words he had seen. Jeff would often have what his parents called temper tantrums. He seemed very upset and frustrated, but his parents could never figure out the reason. They only knew that music seemed to calm and soothe him.

By five years of age, Jeff seemed unusually unaware of other children. His parents worried that he showed no interest in making friends. They thought that friends his own age might help him come out of his shell. But Jeff did not play make-believe games and was confused when, for example, another child poured him a cup of pretend tea. However, he liked to have the attention of adults. He spoke to them in a formal, grown-up manner.

Jeff developed a strong interest in door locks. He resisted any change in his daily routine. At school Jeff screamed when the teacher asked him to finish a task and change to another activity. At other times, he seemed hyperactive and unfocused. He would not sit and listen to a story with other children. Instead, he preferred to wander off to play with the classroom computer. On the playground, Jeff had no idea when other children were joking or kidding around with him. He became the target for some very unkind teasing.

As an adult, Jeff would like to have friends, especially a girlfriend. But he remains socially isolated. He is very good at the technical side of his job as a computer software specialist. But he often irritates customers who are in a hurry with his long explanations of computer technicalities. In general, he is depressed by his lack of job promotions and by his inability to find a girlfriend.

He still has many of the same obsessions from childhood. His interest in door locks has developed into a vast collection, which he carefully catalogs in notebooks. He eats the same food for lunch every day and was very upset when a local shop discontinued his usual sandwich.

When Jeff feels very distressed, he rocks back and forth. He must be reminded not to do so in public. He still lives with his parents, as *he finds it too hard to deal with the everyday demands of living on his own. In his spare time, he plays the piano and works on his lock collection. Jeff has a PDD called Asperger's syndrome.*

You may meet people like Peter and Jeff in the park, in school, in the store, or at work. They don't look very different from other people, yet they behave and communicate in ways that may seem enigmatic, or mysterious. For both Peter and Jeff, their PDDs deeply affect their lives.

Peter's autism has severely impaired many abilities most people take for granted. Autism has left Peter unable to talk and to respond to others' attempts at communication. Having autism has also impaired Peter's ability to understand how people feel. People's tones of voice and their facial expressions have no meaning to him. Whether someone is cheerful or sad, it looks and sounds the same to Peter.

Peter shows little interest in his surroundings. Sometimes he doesn't seem to hear or perceive any of the activities going on around him. At other times, he is clearly overwhelmed by what most people are able to filter out as background noise, such as phones ringing or car horns honking. These sudden noises actually hurt Peter's ears and make his heart pound. He reacts very strongly by screaming and covering his ears.

People with autism can be very sensitive to sound. This boy covers his ears to block out noise.

In general, Peter focuses all his attention on simple objects and activities. He could spend hours flicking a piece of string or splashing in his pool. These repetitive and obsessive habits and interests are called stereotyped behaviors. He also plays with toys, but he does not engage in pretend play. He cannot grasp the idea of pretending that a box is a spaceship or that his small plastic red ball is a huge meteorite streaking the sky. To him, his ball is always just a ball.

All these characteristics—the inability to talk and understand speech, trouble socializing with people, and stereotyped behaviors and interests—are at the core of autism. The characteristics make it very difficult for Peter to have friends and to fit in at school, at home, or in public places. Peter has a severe form of autism.

Jeff's Asperger's syndrome is a different form of PDD. Jeff shares some behaviors with Peter, but he also shows important differences. The differences are in the number of problems he has in communicating, socializing, and behaving. He also differs in the way he expresses these difficulties.

One of the main characteristics of autism is repetitive behaviors such as flicking fingers. This boy lives in a community for autistic adults in Italy.

Unlike Peter, Jeff speaks. His vocabulary is rich, although he mostly talks about computers and locks. He speaks clearly and logically and can sound serious. He doesn't mean to, but he also often sounds condescending—like a "know-it-all." In general, his tone of voice is flat. His voice lacks the ups and downs in volume and stress that most people use when speaking.

Jeff tries to talk to others. But he tends to talk at people rather than with them. His conversations are more like monologues about a specific topic he is fascinated with, such as his lock collection. He does not follow any attempt by the other person to start a new topic.

Like Peter, Jeff has difficulty socializing with people and making friends. But where Peter shuts out other people, Jeff is frustrated by his problems fitting in. He doesn't understand other people's reactions to his behaviors. For example, if he begins to sound condescending, he doesn't understand why the other person frowns or drops eye contact. Because he cannot pick up conversational cues, he finds it hard to alter his behavior.

THE BRAIN

Autistic disorders, such as those Jeff and Peter have, are developmental disorders that affect the brain. This means that the disorders arise when a condition disturbs the process of brain development. The human mind is all the information and stimuli that the brain processes into memories, thoughts, desires, and feelings. Autistic disorders specifically affect those aspects of the mind involving communication, socialization, and behaviors.

People with an autism disorder in any of its degrees of severity have developed a mind that works differently than most people's minds. In consequence, they do not see the world, learn from the world, and think and act in the world in the same way most people do.

AUTISM SPECTRUM DISORDERS (ASD)

If you looked at a large group of people with autism disorders, you would see that some of them have characteristics similar to Peter's. Others would act in a way that would remind you of Jeff. But you would also see many individuals who are not quite like Peter or Jeff. They share some characteristics with Peter or Jeff but to a lesser or greater degree.

Some individuals may be very impaired in their ability to communicate or might not speak at all. But at the same time, they may show only a mild degree of repetitive behaviors. This same person may also have moderate difficulties socially relating to other people.

In the same group, another person might have some trouble being understood or making and keeping friends. But that person might have profound trouble dealing with repetitive behaviors. Each person has his or her unique combination of characteristics. No two people with autism are exactly alike, just as no two individuals in the rest of the population are alike.

The observation that there is a large range (or spectrum) in the severity and combination of characteristics has produced the concept of autism spectrum disorders. The concept indicates that autistic disorders do not always cause profound impairments. Instead, ASD accounts for a wide variation in the degree and type of autistic characteristics.

The American Psychiatric Association (APA) looks to a variety of diagnostic criteria to determine whether a person can be diagnosed with ASD. According to the APA, an individual must show some mild to severe impairment in all three of the following areas: 1) communication, 2) socialization, and 3) repetitive behaviors and restricted interests. There are other criteria to consider, but these three are the most important. This triad of, or group of three, symptoms defines ASD. Individuals like Peter have been diagnosed with the most severe form of ASD because they have profound impairments in all the above categories.

Individuals like Jeff, on the other hand, have been diagnosed with Asperger's syndrome. Asperger's syndrome is characterized by the ability to speak and communicate, although in an unusual way.

People with Asperger also show mild to severe difficulties in socialization, repetitive behaviors, and restricted interests. People with Asperger's syndrome have different levels of difficulty understanding and using social cues. Social cues include body language, facial expressions, sarcasm, jokes, or other subtle forms of communication. Like others in the spectrum, people with Asperger's syndrome show little eye contact while speaking, experience difficulty socializing, and have very few interests. They also have persistent behaviors that may seem unusual to others or that stand out, are often overly sensitive to certain stimuli, and may show some unusual physical movements.

EMERGENCE OF ASD

Parents are usually the first to notice when a child begins showing characteristics of ASD. The characteristics typically appear between eighteen months and six years of age. The disorder is not usually detected earlier because babies typically begin to talk and socialize in their second year. Socialization and communication are two of the main areas of development affected by ASD.

Most cases of the more severe forms of ASD are diagnosed between eighteen months and three years of age. Asperger's syndrome is detected later but usually before the age of six. Asperger's syndrome is detected later because children with the syndrome appear to master the basics of language. Like other children, they memorize whole stories or facts about their favorite object or animals. They begin telling these stories and facts to other people at about the same time most children develop language. For this reason, parents do not suspect a child has Asperger's syndrome until the child's social disabilities become obvious.

Sometimes a child with ASD begins to talk by the age of two. But after that, the child completely or partially loses verbal ability. Later, when the child is unable to socialize and speech does not come back, the child is diagnosed with ASD.

Individuals with ASD are born with their disorder. It is not an illness they catch from somebody else, such as a cold or an ear infection. The disorders are lifelong disabilities—people do not outgrow them and there is no cure yet. However, as children with ASD grow into adulthood, their brains continue to change, just as everyone's brain does. The brain's plasticity, or the ability to "reshape itself," allows for the possibility of improving a range of skills with the help of professionals.

HOW COMMON IS ASD?

In the 1970s, doctors and scientists began systematic studies of ASD. Back then the estimated prevalence (the number of affected individuals in a population at a given time) of ASD was 4 in 10,000 births.

In the United States, an official report published on May 5, 2006, showed the results of two nationally representative surveys conducted by the Centers for Disease Control and Prevention (CDC). In the surveys, parents were asked whether their child had ever received a diagnosis of autism. The analysis was based on reports of 24,673 children aged four to seventeen. From the survey numbers, researchers estimated that as of 2004, autism has been diagnosed in at least 300,000 children in the United States aged four to seventeen.

Genes and ASD

Genes — the units of body chemistry that control inherited traits — play a very large role in ASD. The evidence comes from studies with twins and families. Twin studies show that if one identical twin has ASD, then there is an 82 to 92 percent chance that the other twin will also have the disorder. If the twins are not identical, the chance is about 10 percent. Also, siblings of individuals with ASD have a 2 to 8 percent chance of carrying the disorder. Children with siblings without ASD have less than a 1 percent chance of having the disorder. ASD is about four times more common in boys than in girls, although scientists still don't know exactly why this is true.

Twins Kyle *(left)* and Ian Brown *(right)* are autistic. The incidence of autism in identical versus nonidentical twins points to a genetic basis for the disorder.

This result is similar to current worldwide figures. In 2004 about 6 children out of 1,000 were affected by the disorder, among all social and ethnic groups. Both the U.S. Department of Health and Services and the CDC showed a further increase in ASD prevalence in 2007. Approximately 1 in every 100 children—a total of 673,000 children—were diagnosed with ASD in the USA in 2007.

These statistics show a surprising increase in the prevalence of the disorder between 1970 and 2007. In 1970 ASD was diagnosed in 4 of every 10,000 children. In 2004 the numbers were 6 of every 1,000 children, and in 2007 1 in every 100 children were diagnosed with ASD. This change in prevalence represents a huge increase of the disorder in thirty-seven years. This is dramatically higher than the increase in other brain disorders. Many have asked, is there an epidemic of ASD?

Popular theories among the general public to explain the increase have included the suggestion that autism is caused by brain damage from the vaccine for MMR (measles, mumps, and rubella); from the mercury present in thimerosal (a preservative once used in vaccines); or from allergies, antibiotics and other prescription medications, and environmental contaminants. But no solid scientific evidence supports the theory that any of the above factors cause autism.

In fact, the majority of the scientific community agrees that no autism epidemic exists. Expert Dr. Eric Fombonne at McGill University in Canada has worked in several autism prevalence studies. Fombonne says that one of the main factors behind the rise in the number of cases is that the medical definition of ASD has expanded over the years. In the 1970s, only individuals with the most severe characteristics were considered to have ASD. But later, the definition was expanded to include individuals at the milder end of the spectrum.

www.usatoday.com

USA TODAY

Life

SECTION D

October 5, 2009

From the Pages of USA TODAY

Studies: Autism more widespread, but why?

Rise could be true increase—or not

Anew government survey estimates that more U.S. children than ever have a diagnosed autism spectrum disorder. But the rate varied by sex and racial or ethnic group:

    Boys: 173 of 10,000
    Girls: 43 of 10,000

Hispanic: 103 of 10,000
Non-Hispanic white: 125 of 10,000
Non-Hispanic black: 61 of 10,000
Non-Hispanic multiracial: 71 of 10,000
Non-Hispanic other single race: 66 of 10,000

    —Rita Rubin (Source: Pediatrics)

Statistics experts such as Fombonne remark that it is crucial to differentiate prevalence from incidence. Prevalence is the proportion of individuals in a population who have a defined condition at a given point in time. Incidence is the number of new cases occurring in a population over a period of time. Prevalence is useful to experts who estimate the medical needs of a population and who plan related services for the community with that information in mind. But only incidence rates can be used to study whether the number of cases of any given condition increases or decreases over time.

To fairly compare two separate prevalence or incidence studies, people must be tested using exactly the same diagnostic tests. Experience has shown that when the definition of the condition that is being measured is broadened, then both the prevalence and the incidence numbers rise.

This has happened in the case of autism and related disorders. The original criteria or characteristics used to diagnose autism were much stricter than current criteria. As doctors learned more about the disorder, they realized the tremendous variability in characteristics and severity. They then widened the criteria for diagnosis to include all the forms of autism in the spectrum— including Asperger's syndrome and other forms of autism-related disorders. As a result, more individuals fit the diagnosis of autism than before.

Helen Heussler and her team at Nottingham University in the United Kingdom have found evidence that supports Fombonne's statement. In 2001 Heussler's team reexamined the data from a 1970 survey of 13,135 British children using current diagnostic criteria for ASD. The original survey used strict criteria that only specified "gross language deficits" and "pervasive lack of responsiveness" for a diagnosis of autism. It reported only five autistic children in the whole group. When Heussler and her team used the current wider criteria in the same patients, they found that fifty-six of the children received an autism diagnosis. The tenfold increase prompted the researchers to conclude that the early criteria for diagnosis of autism seriously miscalculated the number of cases.

How Common Is It?

ccording to the Autism Society of America (ASA), autism spectrum disorders are more common than childhood cancer, cystic fibrosis, and multiple sclerosis combined.

In 2009 Marissa King and Peter Bearman at Columbia University in New York reported that changing the criteria for diagnosing ASD substantially affected the number of cases reported in California. But using wider criteria alone explains one-quarter of the increase in prevalence observed in this study. This result suggests that besides better diagnosis methods, other factors may be involved in the increase in prevalence. Scientists have not yet found specific environmental factors that might increase the risk of ASD. However, it is clear that genetic factors are involved in the disorder. Recent research suggests that the age of the parents when their first child is born may be associated with ASD. Scientists are also studying how having a family history of autoimmune disease (diseases in which an individual's immune system does not work properly) might be involved in ASD.

Most scientists have come to accept the wider diagnosing criteria as one of the main explanations for the dramatic increase in the prevalence of ASD. Another important factor has been that professionals and the general public are more aware of the disorders. In spite of the evidence, the question of an autism epidemic remains open for many people. Tony Charman of the Institute of Child Health at the University College London in the United Kingdom has said that there is no clear proof that the number of cases has increased. Yet there is no definite proof that the number hasn't increased either. Research is in progress to find the answer to this puzzling question.

CONTRIBUTING FACTORS

People with ASD may also be living with other complicating medical conditions. For example, ASD is commonly seen with developmental delays (a condition that slows a person's learning and development). Some estimates indicate that about 25 percent of people with ASD also have developmental delays. Other estimates have found the proportion to be about 45 percent. More research is on the way to clarify this point. Epilepsy, a brain disorder that can cause convulsions and a loss of consciousness, is present in nearly one-third of individuals with ASD. In most cases, medications can control and treat epilepsy effectively. Studies also show that many people with ASD experience sleep disorders and depression. Other conditions associated with ASD include digestive problems (such as poor tolerance of gluten, a wheat protein), immune problems such as allergies, and a reduced ability of the liver to eliminate toxins. Treatment of these conditions improves the quality of everyday life but does not cure ASD.

People with ASD have difficulty with the way they perceive their world through their senses. Their senses might perceive external stimuli more intensely than most people. For example, some may be so disturbed by the noise of a vacuum cleaner or airplanes flying by that they cannot tune out those noises. Hypersensitivity to sounds and touch might account for certain behaviors. For example, people with ASD might reject a mother's hug because it feels too intense. They might hit their ears with their hands because they perceive a sound as so loud that it hurts.

On the other hand, some ASD individuals are hyposensitive. The opposite of hypersensitivity, hyposensitivity means that a person perceives stimuli much less intensely than do other people. This lack of sensitivity may have harmful consequences. For instance, some hyposensitive individuals do not react to physical pain as a warning against danger. They may touch a hot stove, for example, and get injured by the heat. But because they do not feel the pain, they are far less likely to seek medical help. If the injury is severe, this can create a life-threatening situation.

ASD: PAST AND PRESENT

Much progress has been made in understanding ASD since its first description in scientific journals in the early 1940s. But researchers know there is still much more to understand. Scientists believe that ASD is the result of a complex interaction between genetic and environmental factors.

No cure currently exists for ASD. The APA has indicated that more than 60 percent of individuals in the spectrum never learn to fully communicate and socialize. Yet with help from innovative teaching

Insiders' Views

Numerous insights about ASD come from individuals living with the condition who are able to communicate their feelings to parents, teachers, and doctors. They speak about the difficulties they face in schools and other social environments.

George, for example, has Asperger's syndrome. At school he faces teasing and peer pressure and he has difficulty learning classroom skills. He wants to get a job and make friends, but it is very hard for him. He's not sure how to make a good impression on people.

People with ASD are also proud of their talents. Tim says his main talents are problem solving, being detail oriented, and wanting to do a good job. He has a bachelor of science degree in business. Greg knows that he's good at reading and creating characters for stories. He's proud of having a very vivid imagination.

June 19, 2003

From the Pages of USA TODAY

Autism now diagnosed early

Red flags for autism

First Signs Inc. says these "red flags" could signal an autism spectrum disorder or other developmental problem and warrant an immediate evaluation:

- No big smiles or other warm, joyful expressions by 6 months or thereafter.
- No back-and-forth sharing of sounds, smiles or other facial expressions by 9 months or thereafter.
- No babbling by 12 months.
- No back-and-forth gestures, such as pointing, showing, reaching or waving by 12 months.
- No words by 16 months.
- No two-word meaningful phrases (without imitating or repeating) by 24 months.
- Any loss of speech, babbling or social skills at any age.

—Kim Painter

and other educational approaches, people with ASD can develop and improve their skills and abilities.

One of the most significant advances in the field has been to help parents, teachers, and doctors better understand ASD. During the first thirty to forty years after the original description of autism, people considered all individuals with ASD to be intellectually delayed and without feelings toward others. It was believed that there was no hope for improving the lives of people with ASD. Some doctors recommended that parents place children with ASD in institutions and forget about them.

The current view of ASD is quite different. While it is impossible to predict the future of people in the spectrum, experience has shown that with intensive treatments, some people with ASD may become more able to communicate and cope in social situations.

It is now widely accepted that people with ASD have a different type of brain that leads to a different type of mind. The ASD brain is structured or "wired" differently than most people's brains. This means that people with ASD perceive the world, understand the world, and react to it in a completely different way. Given the proper stimuli, the brain has the amazing ability to "rewire itself." This has raised the possibility of developing successful therapies to help people with ASD.

CHAPTER TWO

FROM "CHANGELING CHILDREN" TO THE AUTISM SPECTRUM

SAMANTHA'S STORY

Samantha, fifteen, is tall and slim, with bright blue eyes and blonde hair. She works very hard to get good grades at school. She is most successful in classes such as history, where she can use her fine rote memory. She plays the piano very well and enjoys giving performances at school. She's never short for words and makes constant and intense attempts to socialize with her classmates. But she finds that her attempts are usually unsuccessful, and she has few friends.

Samantha is not successful at making friends because she does it in a way other teenagers consider inappropriate. For example, during class breaks and at lunchtime, she talks too much. She's excited to share details about the things that interest her, such as her collection of yarn. But she does not stop and wait for other people to join in the conversation. And when she approaches someone else to talk, Samantha holds the person by the shoulders and talks almost nose to nose. She doesn't understand why people pull back and make excuses to get away.

Samantha also tries to be sociable and make friends by joining ongoing conversations. But her attempts come across as odd and are sometimes disturbing for the group. At lunchtime she makes room for herself at the table by pushing others aside. When others laugh at jokes, she laughs too, often very loudly. But she doesn't always understand the jokes—she just laughs in an attempt to blend in. She realizes that her attempts at making friends are getting her nowhere, and she doesn't know what to do to change it. Her frustration is leading to depression.

Autism and Asperger's syndrome are not new. Ancient myths tell of beautiful but strange and remote children who seem very similar to what modern people would recognize as children with autism. Long ago, people did not understand complex brain disorders. So they imagined fantastic stories to explain these children. Folktales talk of "changeling children"—the children of goblins and fairies that had been left in place of stolen human babies. While human babies were affectionate and eager to communicate, goblin babies were aloof or distant physically and emotionally.

A few legends surround the followers of Saint Francis of Assisi. Saint Francis lived in twelfth-century Italy. He was a Catholic friar (a member of a religious order) and lived and worked with other friars. Among other things, the Franciscan friars took a vow of poverty. They promised to give all their possessions to the poor, keeping almost nothing for themselves. One of the friars, Brother Juniper, was gentle, naive, and very stubborn. Brother Juniper, the legend says, followed the Franciscan teachings literally. He even removed all his clothes in public to give them to a beggar. The other brothers were fond of him, but they worried about his unusual behavior. Modern experts might have diagnosed Brother Juniper with Asperger's syndrome.

In the eighteenth century, detailed accounts of certain individuals seem to indicate clear characteristics of autism. One of the best-known cases is of a young French boy who became known as the Wild Boy of Aveyron. About 1799 villagers in southwestern France noticed a young boy living by himself in the nearby woods. The boy was very dirty and could not speak. Villagers captured the boy and took him to authorities.

A young doctor, J. M. G. Itard, determined that the boy was about twelve years old and had probably been in the woods alone for most of his life. Itard gave the boy a name—Victor. He took care of Victor and recorded lively descriptions of the boy's behavior. At first, Victor did not understand French and did not have a language of his own. Victor also initially showed very little empathy, or the ability to understand other people's feelings. Based on Itard's reports, modern experts believe that Victor had autism.

In the first few decades of the twentieth century, doctors attributed the behavior of these children to personality or mental problems, such as "childhood psychosis" and "childhood schizophrenia." It was not until the 1940s that doctors proposed that the enigmatic behavior was separate from psychosis and schizophrenia. Doctors thought that it was instead a different behavioral disorder that was present since birth. The disorder presented a typical set of characteristics that affected the child's ability to interact with others.

Two Austrian-born doctors are responsible for independently proposing and naming new disorders to explain some children's puzzling behavior. Leo Kanner (1894–1981) described what we know today as classic autism. Hans Asperger (1906–1980) described the disorder that bears his name.

LEO KANNER AND AUTISM

In the 1940s, Leo Kanner was working at Johns Hopkins Hospital in Baltimore, Maryland. There, he had the opportunity to closely observe eleven children—eight boys and three girls, all of whom were younger than eleven years old. The children all had characteristics in common that appeared to constitute a new disorder. The disorder dramatically affected the children's ability to interact socially.

In 1943 Kanner wrote a scientific report about these children. His report described the children's main characteristics. He indicated that the children wanted to be by themselves from the time they were very young—behavior he called "extreme aloneness." They also strongly insisted on keeping their routines and surroundings constant and got very upset if anything changed. Kanner named the syndrome "early infantile autism." The phrase indicated that the disorder was observed in very young children who showed a moody self-absorption and did not have contact with reality. The word *autism* comes from the Greek word *autos*, meaning "self."

In the 1940s, Leo Kanner was the first to pinpoint specific indicators of what he called early infantile autism.

EXTREME ALONENESS

By extreme aloneness, Kanner referred to the children's complete lack of interest in anything that came to them from the outside world. Some of the children's parents confirmed Kanner's observations. They agreed that their children seemed happiest when they were left alone and often acted as if other people weren't even there. If something interrupted their routine, the children either ignored it or reacted in a distressed way.

This extreme aloneness dramatically affected the way the children related to people. It held back their ability to develop emotional relationships. Kanner reported that when the children entered his office, they immediately went after the toys or other objects. They did not pay any attention to other people in the room. They did not seem to be interested in people coming and going, even their mothers. They did not seem to listen to any conversations going on in the room. If an adult addressed the child, the child usually did not respond. In some cases, when the request was repeated many times, the child grudgingly responded to it and then returned to what he had been doing.

In this type of interaction, the child did not look into people's faces or at their eyes when addressing them. If the child wanted to get something he could not get by himself, he reached for an adult's hand and used it as a tool to retrieve the object of interest. Even this interaction usually did not include looking at the adult's eyes or speaking a word.

Kanner indicated that parents reported a similar kind of behavior at home. "Profound aloneness dominates all behavior," he wrote. When the parents returned home, their child did not express in any way that he had been aware of their absence—whether they'd been gone for an hour or a month. Parents said that following a daily routine was not easy for these children. The children learned to follow some house rules and certain orders. But this happened only after repeated insistence from the parents and many outbursts of frustration. After a routine had been established, the child insisted it be strictly followed.

The children Kanner studied also preferred not to play with other children. They preferred to play alone, even when other children were around. They refused verbal and physical contact and did not take part in team games. But sometimes they were clearly aware of the other children's presence. Kanner's children learned the names of the children around them and might even know the color of each child's hair.

OBSESSIVE DESIRE FOR THE PRESERVATION OF SAMENESS

When Kanner described the children as having an "obsessive desire for the preservation of sameness," he referred to the children's constant rejection of changes in their lives. These included changes in routines or the arrangement of furniture. For example, Donald, one of Kanner's children, demanded a specific ritual when he got up after a nap. He would not leave his bed until he and his mother had exchanged exact questions and answers. If his mother did not do this, Donald would scream until the ritual conversation was completed. His temper tantrum was his way of expressing frustration that the nap routine wasn't happening the way he felt it should.

John, another of Kanner's children, became frantic the day his family prepared to move to a new home. John became very upset when he saw the movers rolling up the rug in his bedroom. He remained upset after the family arrived in their new home. But when he saw his furniture arranged in his new room exactly as before, he calmed down. Kanner wrote that John "looked pleased, all anxiety was suddenly gone, and he went around affectionately patting each piece."

CHARACTERISTICS

Kanner's children had other characteristics in common. Most of these characteristics were in the areas of language, memory, repetitive behaviors, and sensory perception.

COMMUNICATION

Three of the children were mute—they did not speak at all. Eight had the ability to speak, but their speech did not convey their thoughts or feelings. They would usually just echo what others said to them—a habit known as echolalia. Sometimes they echoed immediately. For example, if someone asked them, "What are you doing?" they would at once reply, "What are you doing?" At other times, they showed "delayed echolalia." They heard something and then repeated it word for word much later.

Another characteristic of the children's speech was a literal interpretation of words. For example, when John's father said that some pictures were *on* the wall, John corrected him. The pictures, John insisted, were *near* the wall. When someone asked Donald to put something *down*, he put it on the floor. The children did not understand that phrases can have several meanings. They interpreted the words as meaning one thing only.

When the children wanted to request something, they did not use the correct pronoun and intonation. For example, when one mother asked her autistic son, "Are you ready for dessert?" he answered by repeating the phrase. When he said, "Are you ready for dessert?" he meant that *he* was ready for dessert. He did not rephrase the question as an answer by changing the pronoun from *you* to *I*. He also raised his tone of voice at the end of the phrase, as if he were asking a question, instead of lowering it to show that he was answering the question.

ROTE MEMORY

Many of Kanner's children had a superb rote memory. They were able to remember and mechanically repeat large amounts of information. Some of the children were capable of memorizing and repeating long and unusual words. Others repeated the questions and answers of the Presbyterian Catechism, lists of animals, nursery rhymes, a roster of the U.S. presidents, and lullabies in French. But rote memory often lacks real understanding of the memorized material. The children could not apply or use the information in other contexts. For example, a child who knew a list of long and difficult words could not use those words in sentences.

OBSESSIVE REPETITIVE BEHAVIORS

Kanner's children displayed repetitive, obsessive behaviors, such as rocking, flicking their fingers, rolling, or other rhythmic movements. The repetitive behaviors extended to objects. Donald and Charles loved to spin everything that could possibly spin. They jumped up and down in great excitement when they watched the objects whirl around. Frederick also jumped up and down with joy when he bowled and saw the pins go down. Others spent hours lining up blocks, books, toys, or other objects in a specific order. But none engaged in imaginative or pretend play.

SENSATION AND MOVEMENT

Kanner's children had altered sensory perception. Some children were hypersensitive to light, sound, taste, smell, or touch. They reacted to these overwhelming perceptions with tantrums, hitting their ears, refusing to eat, or rejecting a mother's hug. Some children might have also been hyposensitive to pain. And some of Kanner's children had an unusual gait (way of walking) or uncoordinated body movements. Often, though, they displayed well-developed manual abilities—an ease in using their hands.

Kanner published his findings in 1943. The large number of symptoms he presented in his report described classic autism, or the most severe forms of the disorder. He indicated that it was more common among boys than girls and that it was present from birth.

ASPERGER'S SYNDROME

In 1944 Hans Asperger, a psychiatrist from Vienna, Austria, published his report on what became known as Asperger's syndrome. Some scientists knew about Kanner's report shortly after it was published. But a large majority of scientists did not know of Asperger's report for many years. One reason was that Asperger's publication was in German, so some non-German-speaking scientists were not aware of it until 1981. That year British doctor Lorna Wing discussed Asperger's work in one of her reports. In 1991 Professor Uta Frith of University College London translated Asperger's original publication into English, making it available to all English-speaking researchers.

Asperger's first report included four case studies that represented what he had observed in two hundred children he had studied. The name that Asperger originally gave to his syndrome was "autistic psychopathy." Like Kanner, Asperger used the term *autistic* to describe the children's self-absorption and isolation from reality. At the time Asperger published his paper, *psychopathy* meant "having an abnormality of personality." Later, *psychopathy* came to mean "having a severe antisocial personality." An antisocial personality is characterized by aggressive or criminal behavior. But the children Asperger reported on were not psychotic or violent. Because of the negative meaning *psychopathy* took on, autistic psychopathy was renamed Asperger's syndrome.

Independent of each other, Kanner and Asperger had each described a new syndrome that affected children's ability to communicate and establish effective social relationships. Scientists reading Kanner's and Asperger's reports realized that the children had striking similarities as well as important differences.

COMMONALITIES

Asperger's and Kanner's children were similar in many aspects, including gender, some behaviors, and skills and abilities. The details of those similarities are listed on the next page.

1. There were more boys than girls in both groups of children.
2. Both groups included children who preferred to be socially isolated and focus on specific interests. They seemed to lack interest in the feelings or ideas of others.
3. Both Kanner's and Asperger's children had problems with nonverbal aspects of communication. These difficulties included poor eye contact, limited expressive gestures and movements, and inappropriate vocal intonation.
4. They lacked flexible, imaginative, or pretend play.
5. They preferred repetitive patterns of activities or games, disliked changes in routines, and displayed repetitive body movements (such as spinning or rocking). They fixated their attention on specific objects such as trucks or boxes.
6. Both groups of children showed unusual responses to sensory stimuli, such as hypersensitivity to sound or light and lack of sensitivity to pain.
7. Members in both groups showed an unusual gait and other difficulties with motor coordination. However, some were very skilled at certain activities, such as drawing.
8. Some of the children had special abilities with numbers or a very good memory.

DIFFERENCES

One of the main contrasts between Kanner's and Asperger's children was their speech. Asperger's children developed speech before school age. Kanner's children either lacked speech or had an unusual way of using it, such as reversing pronouns or echolalia.

www.usatoday.com

USA TODAY

Sports
SECTION C

September 28, 2009

From the Pages of USA TODAY

Marzo's style is new wave Surf's up

Clay Marzo lives in Maui [Hawaii], looks like a suntanned Greek god, says "waves are toys from God" and rides the giant Hawaiian waves like no other surfer. Marzo, 20, has been diagnosed with Asperger's syndrome.This is a form of high-functioning autism that has given him the burden of total honesty that leaves little room for empathy. It also has given him gifts of athletic skill to go with his sculpted 6-1 [1.9-meter], 175-pound [79-kilogram] body.

"He knows things I don't know," admits 37-year-old, nine-time world champion Kelly Slater. "He knows things that all the guys I'm surfing with don't know." Marzo's unorthodox style has turned traditional competitive surfing on its ear and caught the eye of ESPN. But his Asperger's aloofness has made it difficult for him to compete in conventional contests and participate in sponsors' promotional activities.

Despite that, he has won many events, including the Aug. 19 Association of Surfing Professionals Pro Tour men's qualifier event in Mexico.

—*Sal Ruibal*

Clay Marzo, shown here in 2009, is a rising star in the surfing world. He also has Asperger's syndrome. Marzo, at least in part due to his Asperger's, is most comfortable in the water. And his incredible focus has helped him excel at the sport.

Asperger's children typically had large vocabularies and working grammar. However, they focused only on specific topics of their own interest and had unusual vocal inflections.

From the social point of view, the behavior of Asperger's children was ineffective. Although some attempted to establish social interactions with others, their attempts tended to be socially inappropriate. For example, some started a conversation by standing almost nose to nose with the other person. In contrast, Kanner's children were most of the time uninterested in establishing social contact.

THE AUTISTIC SPECTRUM

At first, doctors recognized only two types of the disorder. Some children seemed to have autism as Kanner described it, while others behaved like Asperger's children. However, when doctors studied larger numbers of children with the disorder, they found many had a mixture of features from both Kanner's autism and Asperger's syndrome.

As research continued, the boundaries between Kanner's and Asperger's disorders became increasingly blurred. It became apparent that the autistic behavior was much more variable than Kanner and Asperger had originally thought.

For example, even though many individuals with Asperger's syndrome have fluent language, some do not. The majority of people diagnosed with severe autism are developmentally delayed. But a percentage has intelligence in the normal range despite the severity of their autism. The disorders were originally described in children. As these children grow into adolescence and adulthood, they keep many or some of their autistic characteristics and make progress in dealing with others.

ASD are currently divided into three major groups:

1. Autistic disorder
2. Asperger's syndrome
3. Pervasive developmental disorder–not otherwise specified (PDD-NOS)

A specific set of criteria or characteristics describe each of the ASD categories above. In general, children and adults with characteristics similar to those described by Kanner will receive a diagnosis of autism. Those who resemble more what Asperger described will be diagnosed with Asperger's syndrome. And those who don't seem to quite fit all the criteria for autism or Asperger's syndrome will be diagnosed with PDD-NOS, or atypical autism.

ASD is categorized as part of a larger group of developmental disorders—PDD. PDD include syndromes that affect an individual's development in different ways. They include:

1. Autistic spectrum disorders
2. Rett syndrome (one of the most common causes of severe learning disability in girls)
3. Childhood disintegrative disorder (CDD) (normal development for the first two to three years of life, followed by a loss of skills by the age of ten)

Childhood Disintegrative Disorder

Individuals with childhood disintegrative disorder typically show a period of normal development for the first two to three years of life. Then, by the age of ten, affected children lose language, social, cognitive, or motor skills.

Rett Syndrome

Rett syndrome is a complex disorder of the nervous system that affects mainly girls. It is present from birth and is usually detected during the second year of life. The main characteristic is loss of the ability to move the hands with a purpose. Instead, people with the syndrome have stereotypic or repetitive movements such as hand wringing or clapping.

People with Rett syndrome are profoundly and multiply disabled. They may have problems with learning, memory, speech, breathing, heart function, and eating. They require constant and intense support throughout life.

The current estimate is that at least 1 in every 10,000 females born worldwide has Rett syndrome. Many experts believe it is one of the most common causes of severe learning disability in girls. Most people with the syndrome have a mutation of a particular gene and are diagnosed through genetic screening.

THE TRIAD

The triad of symptoms is at the core of ASD. However, researchers over the years have seen that impairments in social interactions and communication, stereotyped behaviors, and restricted interests are not the whole picture.

These are pervasive disorders. This means that a person has impairments throughout many characteristics. ASD affects many other aspects of a person's development—for example, sensory perception, motor skills, and the way people think.

SAVANT SYNDROME

The savant syndrome is a very rare condition. Savants have a developmental disability, including autistic disorders, combined with brilliant talents or abilities. The contrast between extraordinary abilities and marked disabilities is stunning.

Savant syndrome is of interest to doctors studying autistic disorders. As many as 10 percent of autistic individuals are savants. This incidence is much higher than in any other disorder of the central nervous system (the brain and spinal cord), including developmental delays and brain injury or disease. In the non-ASD population, the incidence of savants is about 1 percent. Why people in the spectrum are more likely to be savants is still a mystery.

About 50 percent of all individuals with the savant syndrome have autistic disorders. The other 50 percent are not autistic, but they have other developmental disabilities or other forms of mental injury or disease. The majority of cases of savant syndrome occur from birth. However, cases occur where the special skill arises after injury or disease to the central nervous system in infancy, childhood, or even adult life. Savant syndrome is much more common in boys than girls, the ratio being 6 boys to 1 girl.

The word *savant* comes from the French *savoir*, which means "to know." A savant is a "knowledgeable person"—a person who knows a lot of things. Savants usually display their extraordinary abilities in five areas: music, art, calendar calculating, lightning (very fast) calculating, and mechanical or spatial skills (such as creating extremely detailed drawings). Other skills, reported less often, include the ability to speak numerous languages; a perfect sense of passing time without looking at the clock; and an unusually sharp sense of smell, touch, and sight. A savant always has a remarkable memory.

The movie *Rain Man* (1988) brought the savant syndrome to public awareness. It was a box office hit and won four Academy Awards.

In the movie, actor Dustin Hoffman plays Raymond Babbitt, an autistic savant. This character was based on a real person, Kim Peek (1951–2009), who was a nonautistic savant with a massive encyclopedic memory. However, the character and the story are not based on Peek's life alone. Raymond is a composite of savant abilities and autistic characteristics from a number of real-life autistic savants. They include George Finn, who like Kim Peek, can perform amazing calendar calculations. They can provide the day of the week when given any date.

Kim Peek, shown in 2006, was the inspiration for the Academy Award-winning movie *Rain Man* (1988).

Dustin Hoffman spent time with several savants and their families to learn the characteristics of autism and the types of special abilities savants show. For example, Hoffman observed that one savant had the ability to perform large math calculations very quickly. Another savant was able to count, at astonishing speed, the number of toothpicks that fell to the floor from a box. Hoffman wove together the abilities of these and other savants to play the character of Raymond.

Real-life savants have excelled in areas such as music (both playing and composing) and in arts such as painting and drawing. Some have displayed extraordinary mathematical abilities. At the same time, savants may be impaired in their motor abilities. They may not be able to dress or bathe themselves or take care of basic daily needs such as eating and hygiene.

In 1964 the case of the calendar-calculating twins was one of the first studies of savants presented to the scientific community. The twin brothers were autistic and were able to calculate the weekday of each calendar date spanning thousands of years from the past to the future. For example, if someone asked them on what day of the week November 7, 1472, fell, they would be able to calculate the answer (Thursday) quickly in their heads. They also enjoyed entertaining themselves by going back and forth naming large prime numbers (numbers that can be divided evenly only by themselves).

More recent savants include Gilles Tréhin (born 1972) of Nice, France. Tréhin has autism. His savant abilities include learning to master the upright bass (a musical instrument) without instruction. He also has extraordinary artistic abilities. He has created a unique, imaginary city, Urville, drawing it with exquisite detail and perspective. Tréhin can also perform incredible mental calculations. For example, he can immediately tell that a large number, such as 4,187, is a prime number.

Brittany Maier (born 1989) is one of the very few female savants in the world. She has been diagnosed with autism and other developmental disorders. She is also blind. But she has astonishing savant abilities in music. Without formal training, she has perfect pitch and recall. She only needs to listen to elaborate musical compositions once to reproduce them exactly at the piano. She also composes her own music. Daniel Tammet (born 1979) is an exceptional savant and high-functioning autistic man. He lives in Great Britain where people call him Brain Man. He is exceptional because he can describe his own thought process. This is helping scientists to understand how his brain works. Hopefully, this will explain why he has extraordinary savant abilities. For example, he can recite, in the right order, 22,514 digits of the infinite number pi. Pi is the number used to calculate the dimensions of a circle.

(It is usually rounded to 3.14.) It took Daniel more than five hours to recite thousands of digits more. He can also learn languages very quickly. He surprised a live audience after he learned Icelandic, a very difficult language, in just a week.

What causes an individual to have savant abilities together with dramatic disabilities remains a mystery. For researchers, it is yet another example of the complexities of the human mind.

CHAPTER THREE

WHAT CAUSES
AUTISM SPECTRUM DISORDERS?

KEVIN'S STORY

When he was nineteen, Kevin decided to ask for a psychiatric evaluation. He was very concerned about his nervousness and shyness. As a baby, he had lain in his crib for hours laughing at the leaves on the trees outside his window. As a toddler, he was quiet and content and did not protest if other children took his toys. He began to talk at about one year of age, as expected, but walking was somewhat delayed. He developed good grammar, but he referred to himself in the third person until he was about five years old, saying things such as, "Kevin wants a drink."

As he grew up, he would have liked to make friends. But he remained shy and socially isolated. His social behavior made him the target of a lot of teasing. At school he did well in subjects such as Latin and history that require strong rote memory. But he did poorly in subjects that require an understanding of abstract ideas, such as interpreting the meaning of literary stories in English class.

As an adult, Kevin's facial expressions are limited and the tone of his voice is monotonous. He provides information only if asked and responds as briefly as possible.

Kevin does not have repetitive or stereotyped movements. But he has difficulty with his motor coordination, which makes it hard for him to excel at playing sports. He does not swing his arms when he walks, which makes him look uncomfortable.

After graduating from high school, Kevin was in the army for a short time. But he could not take part in marches, parades, and many field exercises because of his difficulty with coordination. He felt clumsy, as if he could not do the right thing at the right time.

Eventually, he was discharged from the army because of his poor motor skills.

Since childhood, Kevin has loved toy buses, cars, and trains. His collection is huge, and he immediately notices if one of them is missing. As a child, he played with these toys for long periods of time. As an adult, he reads books about transportation and goes on trips to see trains with other enthusiasts.

Kevin has worked for years in a routine office job. Although he enjoys his job and his hobby, he's often sad and anxious. He is aware of his social limitations and would like to have friends and to marry. For these reasons, Kevin decided to see a psychiatrist, who diagnosed him with Asperger's syndrome.

THE AUTISTIC BRAIN

The brain is in charge of all human behavior. Scientists have been studying the brain in an attempt to find out what causes autistic behaviors. Because the brain is the most complex organ in the human body, scientists are only just beginning to understand how the human brain grows, develops, and coordinates numerous tasks.

The brain is the organ that perceives, stores, and interprets stimuli, or the information we sense from the environment. It also regulates and coordinates body movements and allows us to communicate with others. The brain and the brain stem (the lower part of the brain that links to the spinal cord) are involved in regulating and coordinating a range of bodily functions. These functions are both voluntary and involuntary, from playing a musical instrument and catching a ball to breathing, digesting food, fighting disease, and keeping the heart beating.

The brain is also in charge of what experts call cognitive, or thinking, functions. These include planning, organizing, and coming up with ways to solve problems. These functions also include recognizing other people and their moods.

The brain's ability to control and regulate our body functions and to create a unique individual largely depends on the structure of the brain. For this reason, scientists have been studying the brain structure and brain activities of ASD individuals. The scientists compare them to the same structures and activities in the brains of individuals without ASD. The comparison is an attempt to find differences that might explain autistic behaviors.

Researchers have not found a single localized brain abnormality to explain ASD. However, they have found that autistic brains are different from other brains in more than one way. These include the way the brain grows in infancy, differences in the structure of specific brain areas, and differences in how various areas of the brain communicate with one another. Scientists have also tried to understand how the minds of people in the autistic spectrum work—how they think.

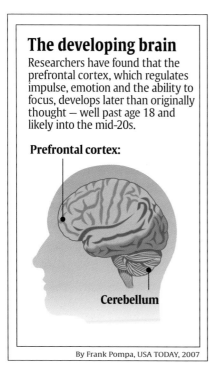

The developing brain

Researchers have found that the prefrontal cortex, which regulates impulse, emotion and the ability to focus, develops later than originally thought — well past age 18 and likely into the mid-20s.

Prefrontal cortex:

Cerebellum

By Frank Pompa, USA TODAY, 2007

GROWTH PATTERNS

The brain of a typical newborn baby grows significantly during the first five to six years of life. When parents take their babies to the doctor for periodic checkups, one of the things doctors measure is the circumference of the baby's head. This is a reliable indicator of brain volume, which indicates normal growth.

Researchers have found that a brain with ASD tends to grow at a different pace than a brain without ASD. At birth, babies with and without ASD have approximately the same head circumference. But by two to four years of age, the brain volume of ASD babies exceeds the average brain by 5 to 10 percent. This is a very significant difference. The phenomenon is called macrocephaly, which literally means "big head." Larger heads correspond to larger brains in the early years of human growth. When children with ASD reach six or seven years old, however, their enlarged brain volume tends to be less noticeable.

Macrocephaly is more common in ASD than in the general population. Considering all ages and levels in the autistic spectrum, about 20 percent of ASD individuals have macrocephaly. In the general population, only 3 percent of people have heads larger than the average.

Macrocephaly does not occur in all ASD children, however. The opposite—microcephaly (small heads)—may also be present in 3 to 7 percent of ASD children. And some ASD children have an average head size, which is referred to as normocephaly. The results of these studies have been confirmed by using modern brain imaging techniques. It is still unclear why autistic brains grow as fast as they do in the early years of life.

DIFFERENCES IN SPECIFIC BRAIN REGIONS

Scientists also look at specific areas of the brain. Certain areas control people's behaviors. Others process emotions, sensations or speech.

THE ASYMMETRIC BRAIN

If you could hold a brain in your hand and look at it from the top, you would see that the organ is divided into a left and a right side. These are called the left and the right hemispheres. The hemispheres are connected by a network of nerves called the corpus callosum. The corpus callosum allows the two sides to work together.

Typically, the left and right hemispheres are not always the same size. Left-handed people usually have symmetric brains, meaning that the left and the right hemispheres are about the same size. Right-handed people tend to have asymmetric brains, with the left hemisphere larger than the right. It appears that the right hemisphere is dominant for, or largely controls, spatial abilities, face recognition, creating visual images, and musical talent. The left brain seems to dominate for language, math, and logic. Scientists have found that some people with ASD have a reversal of their brain asymmetry. But it is not clear how the reversal is linked to the disorder.

THE EMOTIONAL CENTER OF THE BRAIN

The amygdala—an almond-shaped mass of gray matter—is a brain region that has been often associated with ASD. The reason is that the amygdala controls some aspects of social behavior. For example, it allows us to recognize faces and emotions in people. It is in charge of our own feelings, especially fear. It is important for visual learning and memory.

In most children, the amygdala grows slowly until adolescence, when it reaches adult size. But in brains with ASD, the amygdala grows faster and reaches adult size before adolescence. Having an amygdala that grows differently may result in some of the social behaviors of autistic individuals, such as the difficulty or inability to recognize faces and to understand emotions.

The Human Brain

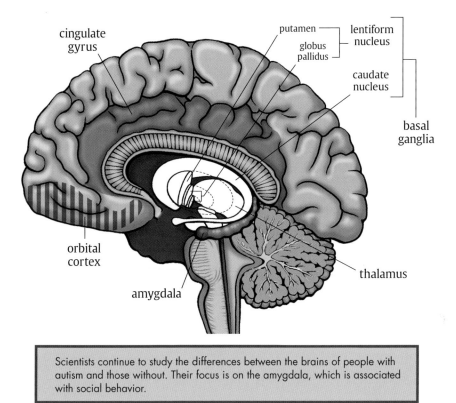

cingulate
gyrus

putamen

globus
pallidus

lentiform
nucleus

caudate
nucleus

basal
ganglia

orbital
cortex

amygdala

thalamus

Scientists continue to study the differences between the brains of people with autism and those without. Their focus is on the amygdala, which is associated with social behavior.

In 2006 researchers at the University of California, Davis, took a closer look at the amygdala in eight- to ten-year-old boys with autism. Their amygdalae were compared to a control group—other boys' amygdalae of the same age but without ASD. The researchers studied the amygdalae after the subjects' deaths. They reported that the amygdalae of autistic brains were about the same volume as in control brains. But the amygdalae of ASD brains had significantly fewer neurons, or brain cells, compared to controls. Scientists are trying to determine why the amygdalae of autistic brains tend to grow faster and have fewer neurons than most amygdalae. In 2010 a group of scientists at the Max Planck Institute in Berlin, Germany, found that individuals with ASD who have trouble identifying faces also had abnormal amygdalae. This supports the idea that the amygdala, the emotional center of the brain, might be involved in ASD.

While some areas of autistic brains are different from most brains, this does not mean that the altered region is the direct cause of ASD. For example, if the amygdala of ASD brains has fewer neurons, does this mean that a reduction of the number of neurons in the amygdala would always lead to ASD? Not necessarily, research shows. For example, Urbach-Wiethe disease results in the destruction of the amygdala, but people with this disease do not present the triad of symptoms at the core of ASD.

Other areas also show differences in ASD brains. For example, the cerebellum of some individuals with ASD has fewer cells than most cerebellums. The cerebellum controls muscle movement and helps maintain balance. This may explain why some individuals in the autism spectrum have an unusual way of walking and poor hand coordination. Besides looking at the brain structure, scientists have studied how autistic brains work. By comparing the function of ASD brains with that of other brains, scientists hope to shed light on what causes autistic behaviors.

THE BRAIN'S ELECTRICAL ACTIVITY

One of the ways brain cells communicate with one another is through tiny electrical signals. Scientists soon realized that measuring these tiny electrical clues would give them an idea of how the brain works.

The brain's electrical activity is measured with a test called an electroencephalogram (EEG). To record an EEG, doctors attach special sensors all over a person's scalp. The sensors detect the electrical output of neurons in the outer surface of the brain (which is the closest to the scalp). The outer surface of the brain is called the cortex. Because the brain's electrical output is very low, it is measured in tiny units called microvolts (one millionth of a volt).

Data from EEGs help scientists study how the brain functions. For this reason, scientists have recorded EEGs in individuals with ASD and compared them with EEGs of individuals without ASD. The comparisons have shown that ASD brains work differently than non-ASD brains.

In one set of experiments, scientists measured the brain's electrical activity of the cortex during sleep. They call this activity background EEG. They compared the background EEGs of people with ASD to that of people without ASD. The comparison showed that as people without ASD sleep, they have greater activity on the front and back areas of the right side of the cortex. On the other hand, when people on the autism spectrum are sleeping, they have increased activity only on the front of the cortex.

In another set of experiments, scientists recorded EEGs while people were awake and performing a cognitive task. One of the tasks was to distinguish between specific shapes, such as a rectangle and a random picture. When people without ASD perform this task, a particular group of neurons on the cortex fires an electrical signal at the same time. Researchers record this brain electrical activity as a gamma band (a pattern of brain waves) in an EEG.

As people practice a task, they get better at it. And when they get better at it, the brain activity changes. The gamma band in their EEG becomes smaller. This shows that fewer specialized neurons have become involved in distinguishing between shapes. The brain becomes more efficient at finishing the task.

In people with ASD, however, this is not what happens. When ASD patients are asked to distinguish between shapes, their EEGs show gamma bands like those of other people. But the gamma bands of ASD brains do not get smaller as the tasks are practiced. Instead, the bands stay the same. This means that a reduction in the number of neurons involved in the task does not occur. The ASD brain seems to be overactive, although researchers are not yet certain how an overactive brain may explain autistic behavior. But EEGs do provide another clue as to the differences in the way ASD brains work.

NEUROIMAGING THE AUTISTIC BRAIN

Neuroimaging provides researchers with a two- or three-dimensional picture—an image—of the human brain. These revolutionary methods allow scientists to look at brain activity at the surface level. They also give scientists a look into the deeper areas of the brain's structure. Scientists use neuroimaging to learn how the brain works when individuals are presented with a stimulus or asked to perform a particular cognitive task. The images' colors show the activity of certain brain areas when a person is performing specific tasks.

Two of the most commonly used neuroimaging techniques are functional magnetic resonance imaging (fMRI) and positron-emission tomography (PET). Functional MRI measures changes in the blood flow within the brain. PET measures the amount of glucose and oxygen used by brain cells for energy. Blood flow and the use of oxygen and glucose are not direct measurements of brain activity. However, scientists have learned that when the brain activity increases, the blood flow also increases. Also, when brain activity increases, neurons consume more glucose and oxygen. So measuring blood flow and the use of glucose and oxygen provide indirect but reliable measurements of brain activity.

Scientists have used fMRI and PET scans to monitor the brain activity of people with ASD while performing tasks that are difficult for them. One difficult task for an ASD individual is recognizing the face of a person he or she knows. In studies, ASD individuals are shown a photo of someone they know. Neuroimaging techniques show reduced activity in an area of the brain called the fusiform face area. In contrast, this area is highly active in people without ASD when they recognize someone's face. Scientists are trying to find out why the brain area involved in recognizing faces works differently in people with ASD.

Another task that is difficult for many individuals with ASD is perceiving body language. For example, a person with ASD might not understand why someone is looking repeatedly at her watch during a conversation. The ASD individual doesn't understand that the other person probably has somewhere else to be and would like to wrap up the conversation. PET studies of people with ASD have shown that the amygdala, the emotional center of the brain, is less active than normal during social interactions.

NEUROTRANSMITTERS AND ASD

The differences between an ASD brain and one without ASD suggest that the ASD brain has a layout of neurons or wiring unlike a typical brain. This in turn alters the way different areas in the brain communicate with one another.

Besides using electrical signals, brain cells communicate with one another using chemicals called neurotransmitters. These are produced in different areas of the brain. Sometimes, neurotransmitters increase brain cell activity. At other times, they inhibit it, or slow it down. In this way, they help regulate brain activity.

Serotonin is one neurotransmitter that scientists have associated with ASD. Serotonin—also known as 5-hydroxytryptamine, or 5-HT—is a neurotransmitter involved in many brain functions. For example, it helps control sleep, mood, and aggression. It also controls how some senses perceive the environment, and it regulates body temperature and appetite. Some of these functions, such as mood, aggression, and sensory perception, are altered in ASD brains. For this reason, scientists think serotonin might be involved in ASD.

Serotonin is produced by neurons located at the center of the brain. These neurons release the serotonin to the rest of the brain. Scientists found the link between serotonin and autism when they studied the amount of serotonin in brains of autistic people. They found that many individuals in the spectrum have reduced levels of serotonin in the brain.

Scientists also studied laboratory animals with reduced levels of serotonin. They found that the animals had autistic characteristics. For example, they slept, played, and socialized less, and they showed increased aggression. This suggested that some of the characteristics observed in autistic individuals are at least partially linked to reduced serotonin levels in the brain. Furthermore, when doctors give ASD patients medications that raise the amount of serotonin in the brain, some of the autistic symptoms improve. The medical drugs fluoxetine and fluvoxamine increase serotonin levels in the brain. The drugs are widely used to control some symptoms, such as aggression and repetitive movements, in people with ASD.

Another neurotransmitter that has been linked to ASD is gamma-aminobutyric acid, or GABA. GABA is a neurotransmitter that triggers an "off response" in neurons. The primary function of GABA in the brain is to tell it to slow down. It works like a brake to prevent the brain from becoming hyperstimulated. Research suggests that if the GABA system is impaired, the brain could be overwhelmed by hyperstimulation of the senses. And hyperstimulation of the senses is one characteristic of many individuals with ASD.

Some individuals with ASD are very sensitive to background sounds (such as trucks passing by) or touch (such as hugs). They become very upset when they hear trucks or feel hugs because they perceive the sensations much more intensely than most people do. Researchers have linked this extreme sensitivity to lower levels of GABA in patients with ASD. Some medical drugs that target GABA, such as diazepam (Valium), have been helpful in controlling some ASD symptoms.

HOW THE AUTISTIC MIND THINKS

Besides studying the physical and chemical changes in autistic brains, scientists have also studied how the autistic brain thinks. Uta Frith has proposed that at least two cognitive processes of ASD individuals work differently than they do in people without ASD. One process is called the theory of central coherence, and the other is the theory of mind.

DETAILS VERSUS THE WHOLE PICTURE

Many individuals with ASD tend to concentrate on details or parts of what they visually perceive, thereby missing the larger picture. In the 1990s, Frith called this fragmented focus a weak central coherence of the mind. The theory of central coherence holds that ASD individuals have trouble integrating, or putting together, pieces of information into a whole.

More recently, doctors of Carnegie Mellon University in Pittsburgh, Pennsylvania, tested the "fragmented focus" ability in individuals with ASD. The scientists showed them an image of a large letter *S* that was formed by the arrangement of many smaller capitalized letter *H*s. The individuals with ASD often identified only the individual *H*s and not the overall *S* pattern, while people with no ASD saw both the individual *H*s and the *S* pattern.

```
HHHHHHHH
H
H
H
HHHHHHHH
        H
        H
        H
HHHHHHHH
```

Other tests showed that people on the autism spectrum use this same visual approach when looking at people's faces. They tend to focus on the nose or the mouth but not on the whole face. This may explain why they often have trouble identifying and differentiating people by looking at their faces. According to the scientists at Carnegie Mellon, the brain of a person with ASD breaks the face's visual information into parts rather than seeing the whole image. And having a brain that provides fragmented information about faces makes it hard for people on the spectrum to recognize the difference between a familiar person and a stranger.

THE THEORY OF MIND

In one study, a group of adults with Asperger's syndrome were asked to look at a number of photographs of strangers. They were asked to assess the age, looks, or honesty of the people in the photographs. A group of adults without Asperger's syndrome took the same test. Both groups responded similarly when judging these attributes. However, the Asperger group scored poorly when asked to guess what the people in the photographs were thinking in specific situations.

A researcher at the Autism Research Centre in the United Kingdom uses images on a computer screen to assess a boy's skills at recognizing facial expressions. People with autism have a difficult time reading facial expressions.

The ability to guess others' thoughts in common situations was also examined in an experiment called the Sally–Ann test. In this test, subjects are shown two figures, Sally and Ann. In the first scene, Sally and Ann are together with a basket and a box beside them. Sally puts a ball inside the basket and covers it with a cloth. Sally goes away. While Sally is away, Ann moves the ball from the basket into the box and closes it. Sally comes back. Where will Sally look for the ball?

To answer this question, the observer must pretend to be Sally. Before about four years of age, most children will say that Sally will look in the box for the ball. They are not taking into account that Sally was out of the room and did not see Ann move the ball. *They saw Ann move the ball, and they believe Sally thinks just like them.* After four years of age, most children will say that Sally will think that the ball is in its original place.

The awareness that other people have beliefs and desires different from our own has been called the theory of mind. It has also been called intentional stance, mind reading, or mentalizing. All terms refer to a cognitive process that allows people to understand someone else's perspective, or point of view. Frith says that children and many teens with autism lack the theory of mind. In the Sally-Ann test, they would think like a very young child and say that Sally will look for the ball in the box.

Many people with Asperger's syndrome also seem to lack the theory of mind. However, as they grow into adults, many may learn to be aware of others' different thoughts. This awareness does not come easily. It requires a great effort on their part.

For many individuals in the autistic spectrum, understanding other people's feelings is as mysterious as understanding their thoughts. They usually try to get around this difficulty by purposely studying people's tone of voice and body language. Some people in the autistic spectrum create rules for themselves or cards with pictures that they can consult to understand and predict people's behavior. For example, a picture of somebody frowning will be accompanied by the description, "upset" or "angry." Next time they see somebody with a frown, they can check their cards to understand what the facial expression means.

IT'S IN THE GENES

What causes these differences between autistic and nonautistic brains? The structure and function of the brain, as well as the rest of the body, are determined by genes and their interactions with the environment. In the case of ASD, experts agree that it is primarily an inherited condition. This means that genes are more involved than the environment in triggering ASD. The evidence for this comes from studies of identical twins. These studies have revealed that if one twin has ASD, the chance of the second twin also having ASD is greater than 90 percent.

Because ASD varies greatly in its forms and because it affects many aspects of development, scientists believe that ASD involves not one but many genes. As many as fifteen genes located on various chromosomes (the structures in the nucleus of the cell that contain genetic information) may be involved. The chromosomes involved include chromosomes 2, 7, 15, 16, and 17, but no specific genes have been clearly involved in the disorder yet. Scientists suspect that more than one gene may be involved in ASD.

Over the years, scientists have studied more than one hundred genes possibly involved in ASD. Many researchers think that the GABA genes on chromosome 15 and the serotonin genes on chromosome 17 are linked to ASD. In 2008 and 2009, four groups of scientists reported that genes for proteins present in the synapses seem to be linked to ASD. The synapse is the place where two neurons, or nerve cells, approach and communicate with each other. Synapses have hundreds of proteins that help to coordinate complex cell-to-cell communication. If synapse proteins are altered in a way that affects their normal function, the neurons would not be able to communicate properly. This might affect the job the neurons play in the brain. For example, if the neurons with defective synapses are involved in the processing of sounds or emotions, then the individual would probably have problems with sounds or emotions. The scientists found that a small number of individuals with ASD have mutations in synapse proteins, such as neuroligin and neurexin. Studying synapse proteins and their role in ASD is a growing and promising field of research.

Genes alone do not seem to be the cause of ASD. Many scientists believe that the genes linked to ASD predispose an individual to, or make it more likely that the person will have, ASD. If an individual has the genes, then the likelihood of developing ASD will increase if certain environmental factors interact with the genes.

April 24, 2009

From the Pages of USA TODAY

Researchers find many genes related to autism

However, variations would explain only up to 20% of cases

Scientists have found dozens of new autism-related genes, according to a study. These genes eventually could help doctors develop better ways to diagnose and treat the condition.

Yet the study also suggests that the genetic roots of autism are quite complicated.

Unlike children with cystic fibrosis, whose disease is caused by defects in a single gene, people with autism may share little in common genetically, says study co-author Stephen Scherer. He compared the DNA of nearly 1,000 children with autism with nearly 1,300 children who don't have autism.

But even the most common genetic changes in his study were found in only 1% or less of patients, Scherer says. That suggests that "most individuals with autism are probably genetically quite unique," says Scherer of the Hospital for Sick Children in Toronto [Canada]. He is one of 120 scientists from 11 countries working on the study, called the Autism Genome Project.

As co-author Stanley Nelson of the University of California-Los Angeles describes it: "If you had 100 kids with autism, you could have 100 different genetic causes."

But doctors may one day be able to use these findings to offer parents an early genetic test to help predict children's risk of autism, says co-author Louise Gallagher of Trinity College Dublin [Ireland].

The study also could lead to new drugs, because it points out new genetic targets, says co-author Anthony Monaco of the Wellcome Trust Centre for Human Genetics in the United Kingdom.

—Liz Szabo

THE ENVIRONMENT AND ASD

Our environment interacts with human genes throughout the whole life of an individual. However, there is a higher chance that genes will be affected by the environment very early in life. Some of the most vulnerable times include the period when the fetus grows in the mother's uterus, during and after birth, and during the first years of a child's growth.

Some of the environmental factors that may cause ASD include viral infections, such as rubella (also known as German measles). If a mother has rubella during pregnancy, her child has a higher chance of being born with ASD. However, most ASD is not related to the mother having a viral infection during pregnancy or taking certain drugs. In fact, the mothers of many ASD children experienced routine pregnancies. The drug thalidomide, used extensively during the 1960s by pregnant women to reduce morning sickness (nausea), has also been associated with ASD. (When doctors realized that thalidomide also caused physical malformations in babies, they stopped giving it to pregnant women.) Scientists at the California Department of Public Health and at King's College in London, England, reported in 2009 and 2010 that advanced maternal and paternal age may increase the chances of having a child with ASD. The report published in 2009 by Judith Grether and her colleagues in California studied all the children born in California between 1989 and 2002—7,550,026 children. Using this very large sample of the population, they found that a ten-year increase in maternal age increased the chances of having a child with ASD by 38 percent. The same increase in paternal age increased the chances by 22 percent. According to the CDC's 2009 National Center for Health Statistics, the average age at which women in the United States have their first child increased from twenty-one years old in 1970 to twenty-five years old in 2006. This is important because the age of the mother plays a strong role in factors that affect the newborn, including birth defects such as Down syndrome.

Some cases of ASD have been linked to complications during the birthing process. For example, Jim and Tom are identical twins with

Asperger's syndrome. Both carry the same genes, but Jim displays a more severe version of ASD than Tom does. Jim has more difficulty communicating and understanding others. He also gets more confused than Tom does. Autism researcher Matthew Belmonte has documented the early and ongoing lives of the twins. He proposes that birth complications may explain the differences between the brothers.

Tom's birth went without complications, but Jim didn't breathe until the doctors provided oxygen. Belmonte proposes that the brief lack of oxygen may have altered Jim's brain development in ways that intensified his Asperger's syndrome. Brain scans conducted in both twins support the idea that Jim's and Tom's brains followed different paths. For example, Jim has a smaller cerebellum, and the left front side of his brain is very large. When Tom, the less affected twin, performs challenging thinking tasks, his brain activity is intermediate. It is somewhere in between that of a nonautistic child and the activity often seen in children with autism. Jim's brain activity, on the other hand, is so disorganized that it does not resemble either pattern.

In this case, it is possible to see how environmental factors may affect the manifestation of ASD. Both boys have the exact same genes that put their brains at risk for developing ASD. However, in Jim's case, lacking oxygen during birth—a very disturbing environmental factor for any newly born baby—may have made his ASD more severe.

REFRIGERATOR MOTHERS

For many years, people thought that cold, uncaring, or abusive parents were the primary cause of ASD. At the time, researchers believed that living through negative experiences caused behavioral difficulties such as those associated with ASD. These negative experiences could include traumatic events such as physical abuse or being raised by unloving or neglectful parents. Kanner and other researchers of his time thought that children developed autism if their parents, especially their mothers, were cold or uncaring. In response, the theory claimed, the children withdrew from their surroundings and seemed to ignore other people. Doctors called these women "refrigerator mothers."

Experts have since discarded this theory. Although uncaring parents can clearly affect a child, they do not cause ASD. ASD is the result of altered genes interacting with the environment. Modern research suggests that the interaction leads the brain through an altered path of development that results in ASD.

OTHER ENVIRONMENTAL FACTORS

Vaccines such as the MMR have been implicated in ASD. However, there is no data to support this link. The vaccine preservative thimerosal, which contains mercury (an element that can cause health problems), was also considered, and some still suspect it causes ASD. No studies support this idea either. The removal of thimerosal from vaccines routinely given to children has not resulted in a reduction of the prevalence of ASD.

Some reports have linked ASD to bowel problems caused by various foods, such as the plant protein gluten. The reports have proposed that gluten and other foods leak through the gut wall into the bloodstream. From

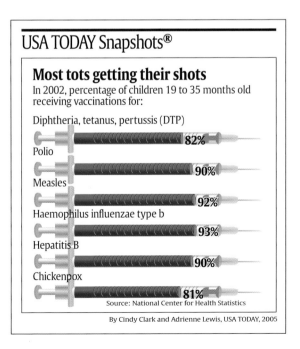

USA TODAY Snapshots®

Most tots getting their shots

In 2002, percentage of children 19 to 35 months old receiving vaccinations for:

Diphtheria, tetanus, pertussis (DTP)
82%

Polio
90%

Measles
92%

Haemophilus influenzae type b
93%

Hepatitis B
90%

Chickenpox
81%

Source: National Center for Health Statistics

By Cindy Clark and Adrienne Lewis, USA TODAY, 2005

www.usatoday.com

Life
SECTION D

December 23, 2009

From the Pages of USA TODAY

Are celebrities crossing the line on medical advice?

People believe them, even if they're wrong

Brooke Shields has talked about her postpartum depression. Michael J. Fox has written about his struggle with Parkinson's disease. Doctors say they can understand why patients sympathize with celebrities and closely follow their battles with serious illnesses.

"It helps people to realize that health problems they have affect even celebrities," says pediatrician Aaron Carroll, director of Indiana University's Center for Health Policy and Professionalism Research. "Knowing that a rich and famous person can have the same problem as you or me makes it seem more fair, maybe. "It also can make it easier to talk about your own problem, because a celebrity has the same issue."

Yet celebrities—who can command huge audiences and sell thousands of books—have a special responsibility to get their facts right, says Bradford Hesse at the National Cancer Institute [Bethesda, MD]. Many doctors say they're troubled by stars who cross the line from sharing their stories to promoting questionable or even dangerous medical advice.

Actress Jenny McCarthy has an autistic son. She has written several books linking

there, they reach the brain and cause damage that sets off ASD. Some reports have tried to link antibiotics and other drugs to the "leaking" of the gut, but no studies support this idea. Still, many doctors suggest eliminating gluten from the diet of people with ASD. This may improve the general well-being of an individual on the spectrum, which may in turn lead to improvements in behavior. However, many experts agree that it's not likely that ASD will be cured through diet.

Other reports have proposed that the immune system is implicated in the development of ASD. The immune system protects autism with childhood vaccinations, even though numerous scientific studies show that vaccines are safe and not the cause of increasing autism rates. For good or bad, research shows that stars exert powerful influence not just on popular opinion, but on public health.

A USA TODAY/Gallup Poll of 1,017 adults found that more than half were aware of McCarthy's warnings about childhood shots. More than 40% of them say McCarthy's claims have made them more likely to question vaccine safety. By swaying parents to delay or reject childhood vaccines, celebrities could undermine efforts to protect newborns and other vulnerable children from devastating diseases, says pediatrician Martin Myers, executive director of the National Network for Immunization Information.

"I worry about these celebrities who confuse people," Myers says. "I don't think they know how much damage they can cause." Studies show that doctors still have great influence. About 68% of people trust their doctors "a lot," according to a 2007 survey by the NCI. Doctors have higher ratings than any other source, such as family, friends, the government, the Internet or other media. As a patient or parent, "you know about your particular situation, but that doesn't make you an expert in the field," says Paul Offit, at Children's Hospital of Philadelphia. "It's part of our culture now. We believe we can be experts by simply looking on the Internet." Explaining complex science—especially in the few minutes allotted on a TV program—is challenging, Carroll says. Audiences sympathize with McCarthy. She says she doesn't need science because she observes her son, Evan, every day. "At home," she writes, "Evan is my science."

"How can you argue with that?" Carroll asks. "It's her child. It's her body. They win." Actress Amanda Peet now works with vaccine groups, encouraging parents to get their medical advice from doctors, rather than celebrities like herself.

—Liz Szabo

the body from diseases. Some individuals with ASD have severe allergies and other immune-related conditions. But as with other ASD theories, no solid scientific evidence supports the idea that immune deficiencies cause ASD.

Nevertheless, individuals on the autism spectrum should be treated by a doctor for any immune-related conditions. Dealing successfully with allergies or other immune-related issues will improve the individuals' overall physical health. This may in turn lessen the moodiness that is often caused by physical discomfort.

CHAPTER FOUR

TESTING AND DIAGNOSING ASD

ALEC'S STORY

S ue was the first to say something about her grandson Alec. Sue asked if there might be a problem with Alec's hearing. "He never turns to look at me when I call his name," she told Alec's parents. Sue offered to pay for the hearing test and then offered to pay for more tests. She began doing research and ended up with a huge stack of papers she had printed off the Internet about children with PDD.

Alec's parents thought Grandma Sue was making too much of Alec's behavior. Alec was their first child, and they thought Sue was exaggerating Alec's lack of interest. Maybe she was even taking it personally. So they made jokes about her research. They found a new meaning for the acronym PDD: Perfectly Delightful and Delicious.

Alec was good at zoning out for long periods of time, and it was very difficult to get him to participate in an activity he did not like. His parents thought that he was just very focused—a good quality he would need later to succeed in school and at work. Alec smiled and laughed, but he didn't talk. Maybe, his parents reasoned, he was just a late talker. But it was also often very hard to understand what he wanted. Sometimes his parents would offer him one object after another, hoping to find the one he was grunting for.

Finally, a scary experience pushed Alec's parents to follow Sue's advice. Alec's parents sent him to day camp, hoping he'd make new friends. But Alec spent most of the day screaming in the doorway. None of their attempts to calm him down were successful. Actually, their efforts seemed to make him even more upset. After this experience, Alec's parents had him tested by a pediatrician. He was diagnosed with ASD.

Parents, other relatives, or caregivers are usually the first to notice unusual or delayed behaviors in a young child. In Alec's case, Grandma Sue was very worried that Alec did not respond when called by his name. Alec's parents saw that he did not like to play much and could not talk. But his parents were not familiar with childhood development patterns, so they did not think Alec's behaviors were serious or out of the ordinary. It took a major traumatic event for them to take him to the doctor for testing.

Testing for ASD is not as easy as testing for other developmental disorders such as Rett syndrome, for example. People with Rett syndrome, who are mostly girls, have multiple and profound disabilities. In this case, scientists have found that most individuals with the syndrome have a mutation on the MECP2 gene on the X chromosome. So diagnosis is done with a genetic test that allows doctors to easily single out the mutation.

This is not the case with ASD. Scientists have not yet identified a single unique biological feature that is always associated with the spectrum. No unique abnormalities in the blood can be detected in a blood test. No specific chromosomal anomalies (irregularities) or genetic mutations can be detected with a genetic test. And no specific tissue or chemical anomalies can be easily tested in the brain. So far, only the triad of behaviors identifies ASD.

DIAGNOSING ASD

Diagnosis of ASD involves a series of tests and interviews that evaluate the presence or absence of certain skills and the severity of certain behaviors. Various professionals perform the tests for ASD. These professionals include pediatricians, who specialize in children's development and in childhood diseases and disorders. Neurologists, who specialize in how the brain works, and clinical psychologists and psychiatrists, who study how the mind works, can also provide an official diagnosis.

The specialist usually meets with the parents and other people involved in caring for the child. The specialist uses questionnaires and the parents' responses to try to retrace the history of the child's development from birth. This is one of the most important aspects of the diagnosis. It helps the specialist see patterns in behaviors and skill levels. Individual interviews may take about three hours. The specialist also meets with the child and observes his or her behavior. If the child can speak and cooperate, the specialist directly evaluates the child through a series of questions. After testing, observation, and questionnaires are completed, the specialist analyzes the information. If the child meets the criteria for ASD, the specialist writes a diagnostic report placing the child in one of the ASD categories: autism, Asperger's syndrome, or PDD-NOS. The diagnosis includes a recommended treatment program.

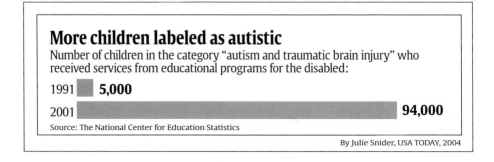

More children labeled as autistic
Number of children in the category "autism and traumatic brain injury" who received services from educational programs for the disabled:

1991 **5,000**
2001 **94,000**
Source: The National Center for Education Statistics

By Julie Snider, USA TODAY, 2004

DIAGNOSTIC CRITERIA

To diagnose ASD, specialists in the United States follow the criteria, or guidelines, described in the *Diagnostic and Statistical Manual of Mental Disorders* (*DSM*). The *DSM* is a handbook for mental health professionals that is updated from time to time with new

February 10, 2010

From the Pages of USA TODAY

Updates proposed for psychiatry's 'bible'

Autism diagnoses at issue

Every 15 to 20 years the American Psychiatric Association (APA) updates its *Diagnostic and Statistical Manual of Mental Disorders (DSM)*. Autism is one of the conditions for which APA is proposing changes in the 2013 edition. The *Diagnostic and Statistical Manual of Mental Disorders*, or DSM, "is a key document," says Stanford University [in California] psychiatrist Alan Schatzberg, the psychiatry association's president. "It determines how mental disorders are diagnosed. It also influences research and what is going to be researched."

For example, proposed changes in diagnostic criteria for autism probably would reduce the number of diagnoses, says Darrel Regier, head of research at the psychiatric association and vice-chair of the DSM-5 task force. Task force chair David Kupfer, a psychiatrist at the University of Pittsburgh [Pennsylvania], says he is skeptical that the incidence of autism has grown as much as recently reported government research suggests. DSM-5 proposes replacing diagnoses for autism, Asperger's, childhood disintegrative and pervasive developmental disorders with a single diagnosis, "autism spectrum disorders." The diagnosis would be based on deficits in social interaction and communication and the presence of repetitive behaviors and interests.

The public is invited to see the proposed changes at www.DSM5.org.

—*Rita Rubin*

information. Since 1994 professionals have been using the fourth edition, text revision, or *DSM-IV-TR*.

In Europe and other areas of the world, specialists follow the official diagnosis described in the *International Statistical Classification of Diseases and Other Related Health Problems (ICD-10)*. The *ICD-10* is published by the World Health Organization (WHO), the public health arm of the United Nations.

DIAGNOSIS: AUTISM

To determine if a child has autism, the specialist looks at all the information gathered and tries to determine if the child fits the characteristics for autism that are described in the diagnostic manual. According to the *DSM-IV-TR*, to be diagnosed with autism, the patient must have six or more of the characteristics listed below. The characteristics are organized in three groups that follow the triad of ASD symptoms.

1. **Impairment in social interaction**

   This type of impairment includes difficulties in understanding and using nonverbal behaviors such as eye contact, facial expression, and posture during conversations. Children with difficulties in this area also fail to develop age-appropriate friendships and other relationships with peers. They show a lack of desire to share enjoyable activities or interests with others, and they show a lack of awareness of other people's feelings.

2. **Impairment in communication**

   Difficulties in this area include a delay in or total lack of spoken language. Children who can speak have clear problems with the ability to begin or keep up conversations. Instead, they show stereotyped and repetitive use of language (echolalia). They also seem to take no interest in age-appropriate make believe play.

3. **Restricted repetitive and stereotyped behaviors, interests, and activities**

   Difficulties in this area include fixations with stereotyped and restricted interests, such as a doorknob collection. There may also be a strong preoccupation with parts of objects, such as the wheels of toys. Specific routines, such as washing hands or cleaning a table, are frequently repeated. And stereotyped and repetitive movements, such as hand or finger flapping or twisting, are present.

For a diagnosis of autism, at least two of the six or more characteristics have to be from group 1. Also, at least one characteristic has to be from group 2 and one from group 3. Another requirement is that at least some of the characteristics must have appeared for the first time before the age of three.

DIAGNOSIS: ASPERGER'S SYNDROME

The criteria for diagnosing Asperger's syndrome appeared for the first time in the *DSM-IV-TR* in 1994. Before then Asperger's syndrome was not officially recognized as a developmental disorder separate from autism. According to the *DSM-IV-TR*, to receive a diagnosis of Asperger's syndrome, a person will show impairments in social interaction as described for autism in number 1. Also, the individual must show repetitive behaviors, interests, and activities as described for autism in number 3. The specialist should be able to determine that the individual's behaviors are causing difficulties or limitations in social settings, at work, or in other important areas of the person's life.

One important difference exists between the criteria for autism and the criteria for Asperger's syndrome. For Asperger's syndrome, the individual must not show a significant delay in the use of language. This means that he or she uses meaningful single words by the age of two and can communicate with clear phrases by the age of three.

The *DSM-IV-TR* also indicates that to receive a diagnosis of Asperger's syndrome, the individual should *not* show a delay in other characteristics, such as being able to get dressed and eat without help and showing curiosity about his or her surroundings.

OTHER EVALUATIONS

Besides performing interviews and direct observation, specialists may recommend other tests to evaluate the individual's general condition. For example, hearing tests would help determine why an individual is not responding to others. If the individual does not have hearing problems, then ASD could be looked at as the reason for the unresponsive behavior.

Specialists at a child's school may also test for potential problems with schoolwork. For example, some specialists may test the child for cognitive, language, and learning abilities. Other specialists may test the child's motor abilities. Although school evaluations are not a mandatory part of an official diagnosis, they are important. They are necessary for the child to receive treatment through state and school districts in the United States.

PROBLEMS DIAGNOSING ASD

In many cases, making a diagnosis of ASD is difficult. The individual may present other brain-related conditions that are separate from ASD but that complicate the picture. These are called comorbidity factors, which means they represent diseases (morbidity) that are present at the same time as ASD.

Aphasia is one comorbidity factor. Aphasia is a speech and language disorder caused by a brain injury such as a stroke. Some individuals with ASD may also have Landau-Kleffner syndrome. Individuals with this syndrome suddenly or gradually lose the ability to understand and use spoken language. The condition can be detected with an EEG. Other developmental conditions include reading difficulties, attention deficit/hyperactive disorder (ADHD), dyspraxia, and dyslexia. ADHD is a condition that makes it consistently difficult for a person to pay attention and control his or her behavior.

www.usatoday.com

USA TODAY

Life
SECTION D

March 8, 2010

From the Pages of USA TODAY

A diagnosis in the book has power to change lives

Public can weigh in on 'Diagnostic and Statistical Manual of Mental Disorders'

From the day she brought her son Jack home from the hospital, Kim knew something wasn't quite right. Kim and her family live a quarter-mile [0.4 kilometers] from the Pacific Ocean in California. Jack, however, wouldn't touch sand. In preschool, the sight of finger paints made him gag. At night, he awoke whenever the furnace kicked on.

Jack is now 9 and an A student, his mother says. He has improved thanks to thousands of dollars' worth of occupational therapy paid for entirely out-of-pocket. The family's health insurance plan wouldn't cover any of it because Jack's diagnosis, called sensory processing disorder, isn't in the American Psychiatric Association's diagnostic manual or DSM.

After a decade spent reviewing the scientific literature and consulting scores of international experts, the psychiatric association last month posted the first draft of the fifth edition of its *Diagnostic and Statistical Manual of Mental Disorders*, or *DSM-5*. The final version is due in May 2013. Families of children diagnosed with sensory processing disorder and therapists who treat them were excited to see a mention of the condition. Although it was not mentioned in the main body of the DSM-5 but on a list of "conditions proposed by outside sources." Says Kim: "I was really happy to hear they're finally taking this seriously."

Inclusion in the DSM carries weight beyond the psychiatrist's office. It influences whether insurers will cover therapy for a condition, whether scientists will pursue research into its causes and treatments and whether the Food and Drug Administration will approve medications that can be marketed for it. As Mary Wylie, a senior editor of the *Psychotherapy Networker*, writes in the March issue, "DSM is the book that everybody loves to hate and hates to love but can hardly do without." Wylie calls it "the one organizing principle standing between the mental health field and sheer diagnostic chaos."

—Rita Rubin

Dyspraxia is poor motor coordination that makes it very difficult for an individual to perform complex motor skills, such as getting exercise or writing clearly. Dyslexia is a difficulty in reading and spelling.

Other comorbidities include developmental delays, tuberous sclerosis, and Tourette syndrome. Tuberous sclerosis is a genetic disorder. People with this disorder have noncancerous tumors in

ASD Diagnosis: More Than Behavioral Criteria?

Many scientists currently believe that trying to differentiate autism and Asperger's syndrome based only on behaviors is not the best approach. The main reason is that far more people have a mixture of ASD characteristics than they have of the pure symptoms.

Many professionals propose that the diagnosis should include a detailed description of other characteristics also affected by ASD. For example, they could include a description of an individual's social interactions; ability to understand others' thoughts and feelings; language skills; sensory and motor skills; and the ability to pay attention, think, plan, and organize. The presence of other disorders should also be included.

Dr. Sarah White from University College London explains that part of the challenge in diagnosing individuals is that a single behavior may have many different causes. A diagnosis also depends on whether the individual is having a good or bad day when under observation. Researchers are working to find the mental, biological, and genetic factors that can be measured precisely enough to lead to a more accurate diagnosis.

many parts of the body, including the brain. The tumors may cause seizures, hyperactivity and aggression, and developmental delays or learning disabilities.

Tourette syndrome is a genetic condition that causes people to have sudden tics. The tics can be uncontrollable movements (such as exaggerated blinking of the eyes) or vocal tics (such as when a person blurts out swear words or repeatedly clears the throat). These disorders can complicate the diagnosis of an individual in the autism spectrum.

Epilepsy is also common in individuals with ASD. It is a chronic (persistent and long-lasting) disorder of the brain that causes seizures, or body convulsions. During a seizure, some brain cells send abnormal signals that stop other cells from working properly. This may cause temporary changes in sensation, behavior, movement, or consciousness. Research suggests that epilepsy is a genetically triggered condition.

Diagnosing ASD in adolescents and adults may be complicated by depression and obsessive-compulsive disorders. Depression often occurs in higher functioning individuals on the spectrum because they are more aware of their difficulties. They become depressed because they want to fit in socially but just don't know how. An individual with an obsessive-compulsive disorder may have repeated thoughts, feelings, sensations, or behaviors that the person cannot stop. An example is excessive, repeated hand washing to ward off infection. These thoughts and behaviors disrupt the person's life, and the inability to control them may also lead to depression.

CHAPTER FIVE

THERAPIES FOR
AUTISM SPECTRUM DISORDERS

SAM'S STORY

When Sam's parents were looking for the best treatments for their autistic son, they felt as if they were going to a restaurant with too many choices on the menu. They were overwhelmed by the number of treatment choices with names, such as TEACCH, ABA, or occupational therapy, that were unfamiliar to them.

They learned that they could not just "get their feet wet" by wading slowly and carefully into treatment. They had to take the plunge to get immediate help for Sam. The therapist explained that Sam's treatment would not be limited to therapy sessions. The whole family would have to adjust their entire lifestyle to accommodate Sam's needs. Sam's parents made a total commitment.

The therapist coached them on how to conduct therapy sessions at home. The family transformed the downstairs of their home into Sam's therapy room. They furnished it as the therapist had indicated, including supplies, and other rewards called reinforcers. Sam's mom put her business on hold. Managing Sam's therapy became her full-time job.

Sam's parents found that other options exist in addition to conventional therapies. In fact, they learned to use many everyday activities to help Sam work through some of his difficulties.

The whole family, including Sam's older sister Joan, enjoy watching DVDs. They have realized that watching movies with Sam is one way to improve his ability to get along with others. At different points during a movie, Joan will mention an actor's facial expression, body language, or changes in the tone of voice. After the movie, the family will discuss what they liked and didn't like. The *conversations provide Sam a chance to express his thoughts and feelings and ask questions.*

Joan thought she was being subtle and casual about the movie discussions. But one day, she realized that Sam was one step ahead of her. As she pulled up the video rental website on the family room computer, Sam looked up from his homework. "I don't want to learn anything this time, Sis," he said with a smile. "Just get something fun."

Receiving a diagnosis of ASD can have a tremendous impact on families. Upon diagnosis, people with ASD and their families learn that there is no cure for ASD and that no medication or surgery can cure ASD. At the same time, a diagnosis can bring tremendous relief. Once a family knows the reason for a child's behaviors, it's possible to take a step forward and look for professional help. Families and caretakers learn that a variety of therapies and medications are available that might improve behaviors as well as social and communication skills.

The level of success a therapy may provide varies with each individual and the level of severity of ASD. For instance, individuals with severe autism and significant developmental delays require constant supervision and long-term specialized care. In many of these cases, current therapies and medications provide little improvement. Nevertheless, therapy is always recommended since professionals never give up hope, and very small changes can sometimes make a big difference in everyday living.

At another place on the spectrum, therapy may provide slight to significant improvements in individuals with Asperger's syndrome who have normal or above normal intelligence. Therapies may improve the individual's abilities to socialize, communicate, and control repetitive behaviors and obsessive interests.

While there is no guarantee of success, the purpose of these therapies is to help children, teens, and adults live more productive lives. Therapies might help individuals fit better into society by strengthening skills in thinking, communication, play, socialization, and independence. To get the best results, experts recommend that ASD therapies start early, be intensive, and be used in all aspects of the individual's life. They require a long-term commitment from parents, therapists, and the ASD individual.

WHEN TO BEGIN?

The American Association of Pediatrics (AAP) states that early therapy for individuals with ASD is crucial for success. Many professionals believe that the reason for this is that intensive early therapy makes the best use of the child's ability to learn. It also helps minimize or reduce harmful or obsessive behaviors such as repetitive movements and self-injuries.

Therapy may start as soon as possible after an individual receives a diagnosis. For treatment of autism, therapy usually begins when the child is between two and three years of age. For Asperger's syndrome, therapy may begin after three years of age. As the child grows, the diagnosis may change. For example, Temple Grandin was diagnosed with autism when she was a child. Through

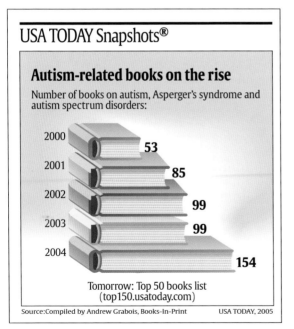

USA TODAY Snapshots®

Autism-related books on the rise

Number of books on autism, Asperger's syndrome and autism spectrum disorders:

2000	53
2001	85
2002	99
2003	99
2004	154

Tomorrow: Top 50 books list
(top150.usatoday.com)

Source: Compiled by Andrew Grabois, Books-In-Print   USA TODAY, 2005

therapy and determination, Grandin learned to control many of the characteristics of her autism. She also learned to use her own talents and strengths. She earned a doctorate degree in animal sciences and developed groundbreaking designs of humane facilities for cattle. She also became a well-known author and public speaker. In 2010 her story was presented in the HBO film *Temple Grandin* featuring actress Claire Danes.

Author Temple Grandin, shown here at the 2010 Emmy Awards, is autistic. She was named one of *Time* magazine's one hundred most influential people in 2010 for her contributions to the public's understanding of autism.

Even though experts agree that the earlier the intervention, the better, Lorna Wing remarks that therapies can bring improvements at any age. Teens and adults should not be discouraged about beginning therapy later.

EFFECTIVE THERAPIES

A long list of traditional and alternative (nontraditional) therapies is available for treating ASD. No one single treatment on the list would help all individuals in the spectrum, however. Each individual is unique and has his or her own strengths and weaknesses. In each case, the individual's most severe impairments *and* his or her strengths have to be carefully considered at the time of selecting a therapy program.

U.S. researchers Geraldine Dawson and Julie Osterling surveyed a number of ASD therapy programs and determined that effective programs have the following characteristics:

1. The programs focus on building the strengths and improving the weaknesses of the person with ASD. For example, the therapist may encourage a child with strong rote memory to use it at school to get good grades (which increases confidence). The same child may not speak, so the therapist may help the child use the computer to communicate.

2. The programs feature an environment that is very structured and has high levels of one-on-one support. For example, having a regular routine at home and at school helps individuals with ASD. They know what will happen each day, which lessens stress and anxiety.

3. The programs emphasize teaching functional skills. For example, they teach how to follow daily routines independently (such as how to take a bath and brush teeth properly), how to ask for things by pointing at them instead of screaming, and how to make choices by saying "yes" or "no."

4. The programs require parents, teachers, and therapists to work together. Consistently teaching and reinforcing strategies at home, at school, and at the therapist's office help individuals with ASD improve their lives.

5. The programs support transitions. As the child grows or as the teen moves into adulthood, his or her strengths and weaknesses will change. Any successful program must adapt to the changes in an individual's life to continue helping that person live effectively.

6. The programs are intensive, meaning that therapies are usually daily and take many hours.

TREATMENT OPTIONS

Some treatments have become very popular for individuals with ASD. They include treatments based on behavior, therapy, and education.

APPLIED BEHAVIOR ANALYSIS

Applied behavior analysis (ABA) is based on the idea that therapists can use their understanding of principles of behavior to teach ASD individuals. ABA is supported by more scientific research than any other treatment for ASD. More than thirty years of research have demonstrated that ABA methods are effective in reducing inappropriate ASD behavior and encouraging positive skills.

One of the techniques ABA uses to teach new skills to children with ASD is called discrete trial training. It uses a reward system. For example, to teach Ted to respond to his name, the therapist will say Ted's name and wait a certain amount of time for him to respond. If Ted responds, the therapist rewards him with a favorite food or toy. If Ted does not respond with the appropriate behavior, the reward is withheld. No punishment is used.

The idea behind ABA is that rewarded behavior will be repeated. Repetition is essential for the brain to learn new behaviors and skills. So the therapist gives the child many opportunities during a session to demonstrate the positive behavior.

ABA also teaches play, social communication, and relationship-building skills through other techniques. For example, a child may learn a new skill through peer modeling—imitating other children in the session or modeling behavior on theirs. Or a child may learn the schedule of daily activities (such as the steps to follow for brushing teeth) by looking at the sequence of events depicted in cards or on a poster.

Therapists encourage parents to be involved in their child's treatment by including what they learn in ABA class in daily life. For example, if the child learns to wave good-bye in an ABA session, the child should also use this behavior in a real-life situation, such as when a parent leaves the house. Therapists and parents carefully record the child's progress in written reports. They review the records often so therapy can be changed to meet the child's specific needs.

OCCUPATIONAL THERAPY

Despite its name, occupational therapy (OT) is not only about teaching occupational, or job, skills. It is a program to help ASD children become skillful in all areas of their lives. This includes taking care of themselves, playing, socializing, and communicating.

OT can help children in the autism spectrum better coordinate their body movements. Occupational therapists may use swings, trampolines, climbing walls, and slides to help a child improve physical skills. OT also works at improving fine motor skills, such as writing and drawing. And OT techniques may help individuals cope with other physical discomforts. For example, by wearing a

A therapist works with children with autism at a school in China in 2010. Occupational therapy helps autistic children improve fine motor skills and may ease physical discomforts.

heavy vest or by applying pressure on the joints, an individual may overcome the dislike of hugs.

Occupational therapists may also provide sensory integration therapy (SIT). The goal of SIT is to help individuals more effectively perceive and process the information they receive through their senses. Through games, exercises, and play, the individual learns not to overreact to certain sounds, textures, or visual stimuli, nor to underreact to pain.

TEACCH

Treatment and Education of Autistic and Related Communication Handicapped Children (TEACCH) was developed at the University of North Carolina's School of Medicine in the 1970s. It uses a variety of techniques to create a custom-made teaching program for each individual.

TEACCH provides evaluations, parent training and support, play groups, counseling, and employment support. The goal of the program is that an ASD individual will learn the communication, social, and overall functional skills to reach their full potential. They will live more effectively at home, at school, at work, and in the community.

SOCIAL SKILLS TRAINING

The goal of social skills training (SST) is to help individuals with ASD make friends, establish relationships, and have appropriate social interactions. A facilitator (such as a psychologist or a special education teacher) usually runs the SST sessions. Parents are encouraged to attend and learn to do the same at home.

The facilitator uses role-playing, games, discussions, and stories to help individuals with ASD. "Social stories" is one technique that has proven very useful to teach social skills. Social stories are short narratives that describe children's or teens' behavior in specific situations. For example, a story about how to share toys has a child asking politely and saying "thank you." This technique seems to work because many people in the spectrum understand behaviors better from step-by-step pictures rather than in words.

Video modeling works much the same way as social stories, but as the name indicates, it uses videos to show the desired behavior. The facilitator may work one-on-one with the individual. Sometimes, to model appropriate play behavior, the facilitator coordinates play situations between a child with ASD and same-age children who do not have ASD.

SPEECH AND LANGUAGE THERAPY

Speech and language therapy (SLT) helps individuals with ASD communicate more effectively both verbally and nonverbally. The purpose of the exercises is to teach children to form words by speaking. Sometimes, therapists use other forms of communication, such as sign language, keyboards, or pictures.

The therapist may also teach individuals how to begin and maintain a conversation. For example, the therapist may teach them to introduce themselves by saying their name first and then asking the other person's name. Or they teach individuals to try to keep eye contact when addressing the other person and to not interrupt when the other person is speaking. The therapist may work one-on-one with the individual or work with small groups.

MEDICATIONS

Although no medications cure ASD, some may be prescribed to help reduce specific behaviors. Some medications may help manage hyperactivity, aggression, and obsessive or fixated preoccupations. Other medications may help to manage attention disorders, anxiety, or depression. By helping to manage behaviors and other conditions that interfere with the individual's life, medications help increase the benefits of other therapies.

Examples of medications most frequently used for individuals with ASD include SSRIs (selective serotonin reuptake inhibitors), antiseizure medications, and neuroleptics. SSRIs increase the levels of serotonin in the brain, which has been shown to help reduce some aggressive behaviors. Antiseizure medications help reduce convulsions. Neuroleptics are chemicals that reduce nerve activity and produce a calming effect. Some ASD individuals seem to benefit from the use of stimulants—drugs that increase alertness.

The use of all medications must be carefully supervised by a doctor and by parents. Medications may have side effects and may interact with one another. For this reason, it is recommended that parents keep written records of all the medications taken by an ASD child. Doctors also recommend that parents write down the behaviors observed after introducing a new medication. For example, parents may record changes in the number of tantrums per day, sleep behaviors, the ability to focus, or harmful behaviors such as self-injuring. If parents notice changes in their child's behavior after introducing a new medication, they should contact their doctor immediately.

OTHER THERAPIES

Parents often use alternative therapies to try to improve the most severe symptoms in their ASD child. These therapies are not widely accepted by the medical community. The main reason is that very few or incomplete scientific studies support claims that these treatments will improve ASD symptoms. In spite of the uncertainty that they will work, many parents use them.

John W. Harrington and his colleagues reported in 2006 the results of a survey in which 150 parents from New York and New

February 19, 2007

From the Pages of USA TODAY

Autistic kids can be helped; For one boy, fast action brings 'amazing progress'

I'm writing about Nathan today because I wrote about him once before, in 2003, when he was 2 and was diagnosed with severe autism. In the story, Nathan's parents, Nicole and Gary, described a child who "screams when he is frustrated, spins in circles to entertain himself and bangs toy cars against the wall."

Despite glimmers of progress, Gary feared a future in which Nathan "never really talks and is always the way he is now: infantile." That was the last I heard about Nathan until a few weeks ago, when I got an e-mail from his mother.

"He has made amazing progress," she wrote. I called Nicole and heard what she and her husband say is a story too seldom told. It's the story of a child with autism who gets the help he needs and makes thrilling gains. But he is neither cured of his autism nor revealed to be an autistic "savant," wowing the world with musical, mathematical or artistic genius.

"You don't hear much about the

Jersey were asked questions about the treatments their ASD children received. About 51 percent of the parents responded to the survey. Almost all the parents, about 95 percent, indicated some use of alternative medicines. These nontraditional therapies had been recommended by a physician or a nurse in 44 percent of the cases.

Some nontraditional therapies, such as using the hormone secretin, seemed to be helpful at first. But then scientists began to study its effect carefully. They discovered that there were no real differences between individuals receiving secretin and control groups (groups of patients not given the drug in question).

Nathans of the world," Nicole says.

Nathan, she says, isn't composing symphonies and does not entirely blend in with his classmates. But thanks to years of intensive speech, behavioral, play and occupational therapy—and an intelligence his parents suspected from the start—Nathan is doing things they did not think possible back in 2003. Among them:

- He rides the same bus as the other kids in the neighborhood.
- He attends the same kindergarten, with an aide. (He goes to a special-education class for half a day, too.)
- He reads and writes and shows a talent for math.
- He talks. Though he does not keep up a long conversation. He can ask questions and tell his parents what he wants to eat, where he wants to go and more.

"About a year ago, he said 'I love you, Mom' for the first time," Nicole says. Gary, a cardiologist, says simply, "He's a very loving boy." He speaks proudly of the day the family was out hiking, an activity that seems to calm and center Nathan. When their son saw another child fall along the trail: "Nathan walked over and said, 'Are you OK?'" It was a nice show of empathy for any young boy, but it was a true sign of growth for Nathan. Nicole says Nathan remains "mildly or moderately autistic," though he is considered "high-functioning."

Nathan's family know that they are fortunate in some ways. They've been able to pay "thousands and thousands" of dollars for private therapies, Gary says. And Nathan went to an excellent, specialized preschool, something that doesn't even exist in many places.

They also know that Nathan still may never do many of the things his two brothers and his sister will do. But Gary says he hopes other parents will see the hope in Nathan's story. "You get this diagnosis and you just cannot see how it's going to get better," he says. "But it does get better."

—Kim Painter

Another alternative therapy is chelation. Chelation therapy tries to chelate, or eliminate the chemical effects of, metals such as mercury or cadmium. Humans need some metals, such as zinc, in small amounts. But humans may ingest more harmful levels of metal through environmental pollution. Some people have proposed that a buildup of these metals in the body might cause ASD. But chelation therapy has not improved the core autistic symptoms.

Specialists strongly recommend that parents of ASD children discuss any traditional or nontraditional therapies with their doctor before using them. The use of these and other alternative therapies is a matter of continued debate among specialists and parents.

WHERE TO RECEIVE TREATMENT

People with ASD may receive treatment in a variety of settings. Determining the most appropriate setting will depend on the severity of the condition and the age of the individual. For example, treatment for preschool children may include at-home therapies with a parent. Or a therapist may work with the child during an office visit. These therapies may be combined with attending a regular preschool part-time. In this case, it would be necessary to have an assistant at the school to work one-on-one with the ASD child. Therapies may also take place at special educational centers with a staff of ASD specialists.

A therapist works with a ten-year-old autistic boy in his home. The options for treatment depend on where a person lives and are becoming more available everywhere.

Secretin's Story

Secretin is a hormone, a type of chemical the body produces to help it function. Secretin works in the gastrointestinal, or digestive, system. Secretin's role in the gut is to increase the production of digestive fluids in organs such as the pancreas, the stomach, and the liver.

In 1998 researcher Karoly Horvath and his colleagues at the University of Maryland were using secretin in three individuals with autism. But they were not using it to treat autistic symptoms. They were using it to understand what caused digestive complaints. If the problems were caused by a lack of digestive fluids, then secretin, the doctors reasoned, might be able to eliminate the complaints. The doctors were surprised when they noted an unexpected effect of secretin. Some of the autistic symptoms, such as eye contact, alertness, and speech, improved.

This result encouraged thousands of parents to give their autistic children secretin. But many scientists and doctors felt that Horvath's successful results were based on the experiences of just three people. Would the result be the same if hundreds or thousands of children were tested?

From 1999 to 2005, other scientists studied secretin's effect on ASD symptoms in many individuals. In these more extensive tests, researchers found that secretin did not affect ASD symptoms. Secretin is not currently recommended for treatment of ASD.

A teacher works with autistic children in a mainstream school in the United Kingdom. Many mainstream schools have therapy sessions for autistic students. Classes such as art therapy help autistic children express themselves and tap into their imaginations.

Older children and teens with ASD may be able to attend mainstream schools. In this setting, the children share classes with non-ASD students. They would also receive specific therapy sessions for their particular difficulties and assets. The sessions would take place in school, after school, at home, or in the therapist's office.

A DAY IN TOM'S LIFE

Tom is two years old and has been diagnosed with an autistic disorder. He does not speak and understands very little language. He has poor eye contact, does not know how to interact with others, and shows delayed motor skills.

Being so young, most of his therapies are either conducted at home or at the therapist's office. His therapies work to improve his ability to communicate using words and body language. He also gets therapy to improve his motor skills. He participates in the following treatments:

1. ABA—40 hours/week at home (about 5 to 6 hours every day, with breaks)
2. Speech therapy—1 hour each week at home
3. Occupational therapy—1 hour each week at the occupational therapist's office
4. Dietary intervention—a gluten-free diet and vitamin therapy
5. Toddler gym class—45 minutes each week on Saturday

To fulfill this program, Tom has a busy daily schedule. Here is what Tom does on Wednesdays:

9:00 to 11:00 A.M.—ABA
11:30 to 12:00 P.M.—speech therapy
12:00 to 12:30 P.M.—a gluten-free lunch at home
12:30 to 2:30 P.M.—ABA
2:30 to 3:00 P.M.—a gluten-free snack and nap at home
3:00 to 5:00 P.M.—ABA
5:30 to 6:00 P.M.—occupational therapy
6:30 to 7:00 P.M.—a gluten-free dinner at home
7:30 P.M.—bedtime

Every day of the week has a set schedule, and Tom's parents make sure to follow it. Changes in the daily schedule are usually very disturbing to individuals in the autistic spectrum and may prompt tantrums or anxiety. But a strong daily routine provides consistency and predictability. Tom knows what will happen each day. This helps Tom stay calm and follow the routine, and in the long term, it may also improve his abilities.

In ABA sessions, the therapist is teaching Tom to say his name. Tom does not seem to care about getting food treats as rewards. But toy airplanes catch his attention. The therapist offers a small airplane as a reward if Tom responds saying his name when the therapist asks. If Tom does not make eye contact, the therapist gently turns Tom's head until their eyes meet. They repeat this routine a few times, take a small break, and repeat it again for the remainder of the session.

Tom is also learning basic skills, such as brushing his teeth, by looking at a sequence of pictures the therapist shows him. The first picture shows a boy standing in front of a sink. The second shows the boy opening the tube of toothpaste, and the third one shows the boy placing a small amount of toothpaste on the toothbrush. The final pictures show the boy closing the toothpaste tube, brushing his teeth, and rinsing his mouth and the toothbrush.

Breaking down a routine into simple steps and showing those steps with pictures is one strategy for teaching children with ASD a new routine. Many people of all ages with ASD seem to learn better using pictures than with oral or written instructions. After Tom learns the toothbrushing routine in his therapy session, he finds the

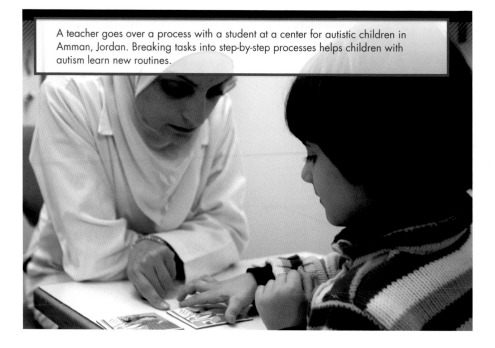

A teacher goes over a process with a student at a center for autistic children in Amman, Jordan. Breaking tasks into step-by-step processes helps children with autism learn new routines.

same sequence of pictures in his bathroom at home. This reinforces what he has learned with his therapist.

Tom's parents also use the picture strategy to show Tom what events he can expect every day. When a change cannot be avoided, Tom's parents use pictures to show him what will happen instead. They reassure him that the change is temporary and that they'll be back on schedule soon.

A DAY IN MARTY'S LIFE

Marty was diagnosed with autism when he was three. Now, at fourteen, he no longer fits the original diagnosis. His diagnosis has been changed to Asperger's syndrome. He uses complete sentences to communicate and has learned many everyday skills, including remembering to make eye contact with others. Nevertheless, Marty is not good at reading facial and body expressions. This leads him into difficulties getting along with his teenage sisters, who do not have ASD.

Marty often follows his sisters around the house talking about the historical facts he has memorized. He does not recognize the boredom or irritation on their faces. Marty also doesn't get why they push him away when he sits too close or when he talks to them a fraction of an inch away from their faces.

He has also found himself in trouble for his overly literal interpretations of what people tell him. In one incident, his sister May had been waiting for weeks for a phone call about a job she had applied for. When the call came, Marty answered the phone. The caller asked, "Hello, is May there, please?" Marty looked around the living room and saw that she was not there (she was in the kitchen). He answered, "No, sorry," and put the phone down. May came into the living room and asked if the call was for her. She got very angry when Marty told her what happened.

www.usatoday.com

USA TODAY

Life

SECTION D

June 10, 2010

From the Pages of USA TODAY

Program helps disabled kids express themselves through art

State of the Art is an exhibition of how obstacles can be overcome

Fifty-one kids ages 5 to 15 have their artwork displayed in State of the Art, an exhibit that's part of the 2010 VSA International Festival and features artwork from artists with disabilities. The All Kids Can . . . CREATE! program, sponsored by VSA—formerly known as Very Special Arts—and CVS Caremark received more than 5,500 entries from children nationwide with disabilities including autism, dyslexia and cerebral palsy.

This is the first year that artwork from one student in each state and the District of Columbia was selected to be in the third annual exhibit. The artwork will be on display in Union Station in Washington, D.C., until Saturday. It then will travel throughout the USA in a two-year exhibition (dates and locations not yet final).

Amanda, 14, who has Asperger's syndrome, a form of autism that affects communication and social skills, painted Oklahoma's state bird—the scissor-tail—with acrylic paint. Amanda started painting at age 7 because she found it helped her concentrate.

"Amanda was just a rowdy little girl, and couldn't stay focused very well, and so the children didn't really want to be around her," says her mother, Sherry. "But when they learned she could paint they saw her through different eyes, and they were more accepting of her."

The children and their families gathered Tuesday for a ribbon-cutting ceremony and to admire one another's work. "A lot of these kids are really inspirational—how they just go beyond their disabilities and they make it into abilities by showing how they can do their different types of artwork," Amanda says.

"I think they need opportunities to do music and art just like everybody else," VSA Ambassador Jean Kennedy Smith says. "And any difficulties that came up—as far as ability and so forth—can be conquered."

—Stephanie Steinberg

May and Marty argued for a couple of hours until their mother came home and heard about the incident. Their mom tried to explain to Marty what he should do instead of responding in literal terms to such questions. She also convinced May that Marty does not do such things on purpose and that getting angry doesn't solve the problem. Then she helped May track down the man who had called about her job.

At Marty's age, good social skills are very important. In addition to interacting with school peers and his sisters, Marty has become interested in girls. To help Marty improve all the skills a teenager needs, his parents have found a therapist they can trust. They have also talked to other parents of teenagers with Asperger's syndrome.

Marty's therapies are not as structured and rigorous as were Tom's. Nevertheless, Marty follows a more rigorous daily routine than his sisters do. Marty has a tendency to feel overwhelmed by sounds in certain environments. For example, the school lunchroom is loud with voices and noises such as dragging chairs and clashing trays. Marty gets anxious in the lunchroom and begins flapping his fingers. The occupational therapist who works with Marty at school has helped him find a solution. Marty has learned to control the overwhelming feeling by having his lunch in a quiet room away from the racket of the lunchroom.

Marty has a difficult time with handwriting because he has limited motor skills. It takes him a long time to write assignments. He's such a perfectionist that he does not finish until each piece of work is done exactly as he likes it. As a result, he rarely finishes his classwork on time. He gets very upset when the teacher asks for it and he's not finished yet. It seemed to the teacher and the school therapist that Marty needed another way to do his classwork. He needed something that was more practical and satisfied his need for perfection. They taught Marty to use a personal computer. Although it took him time and effort to learn keyboard skills, with patience and practice he succeeded.

Some of the therapies Marty enjoys the most occur outside the school setting. For example, playing team sports helps Marty improve his motor skills. But being in the school gym with many screaming classmates was overwhelming to him. Marty benefited more from practicing an individual sport in a quieter environment. He began swim therapy after school to develop basic motor skills in the water, such as floating. Marty found that he liked being in the water, and his skills improved in time. He moved on to learning swimming skills. The swim coach worked with the occupational therapist to make sure they concentrated on particular muscle groups.

In some coastal communities, autistic children can participate in a program called Surfers Healing. Many autistic children find surfing and other water activities calming.

To help Marty improve his social skills, he attends a social skills group three times a week. The group is small—no more than six people at a time—and the sessions are structured. This means that the therapist writes down the activities for each day for the group. The rules of behavior when in session are also clearly written in list form and posted on the wall of the room.

In the sessions, Marty practices recognizing facial expressions and body language with the help of pictures and videos. For example, the therapist shows the group a photo of a person. He asks the students to look at the person's face and find clues for the type of feeling expressed, such as a frown for angry, lips curved up for happy, or half-closed eyes for tired. In these classes, Marty also learns social manners, how to start and carry a conversation, and how to understand figures of speech.

Marty discovered that writing stories about his daily activities helps him organize his thoughts. It takes him hours to complete a short story, even on the computer, but he knows he has to finish it. The rule is that after one of his parents reads Marty's story and helps him edit it, Marty can turn it in for school credit. It gives Marty personal satisfaction and a feeling of accomplishment when his teacher accepts his hard work and rewards him with credit.

Other activities that have helped Marty are art and crafts classes and martial arts such as tae kwon do. Marty enjoys painting, and it has a calming effect on him when he is stressed out. In tae kwon do classes, the activities are very structured and the rules are clearly defined. He is expected to pay strict attention and show respect for his teacher and classmates. This has helped Marty develop self-confidence, self-discipline, and self-control. He felt especially good after being rewarded with a rank promotion. Marty and his parents hope these activities will help Marty grow into a self-sufficient adult.

CHAPTER SIX

COPING AND LIVING WITH ASD

ETHAN'S STORY

When Ginny found out that she and her husband, Mitch, were expecting their first child, she was beyond excited. They had waited a long time for a baby, and Ginny wanted to be as prepared as possible. She wanted to be a great mother and provide a happy, healthy environment for her child. Throughout her pregnancy, she read book after book about childbirth, nutrition, child development, and early education. She and Mitch discussed all their plans for parenthood.

Ginny and Mitch's baby, Ethan, arrived after a trouble-free pregnancy. Ginny settled into her new role as a mom. But by the time Ethan was about eighteen months old, Ginny knew something was wrong. She knew that he wasn't hitting all the developmental goals, such as babbling and sitting up on his own, on schedule. She also knew that little things about his behavior didn't seem right. He didn't cry when he hurt himself. He didn't wave or smile back at people. He often didn't want to be held by his parents. She and Mitch decided to consult a specialist.

When a developmental pediatrician diagnosed autism, Ginny just concentrated on hearing what the doctor was saying. But when she and Mitch got home, they felt overwhelmed. They knew the diagnosis would change every aspect of their lives. All the preparations and plans they'd made for Ethan hadn't prepared them for this. Ginny half-joked that now she'd have to read a whole new set of books. The family would also have to consult with doctors, therapists, and educators. They'd have to find other parents of kids with autism who could share ideas and support. But Ginny and Mitch's goal would be the same—to provide a happy and healthy home for Ethan.

COPING WITH A NEW DIAGNOSIS

"Your child has an autistic spectrum disorder." Hearing these seven words can make parents feel anxious, confused, guilty, and often angry. They might think, *Why my child?* Some parents don't even know what ASD is. Susan Dodd is an Australian expert on autistic disorders. She recommends the following steps for parents and families in which a child or teen has just received a diagnosis of ASD.

Step 1: Prepare yourself to make the best decisions for the child. It's important for the child to begin therapy and an organized and predictable lifestyle as soon as possible. Experience has shown that to make the best decisions, parents must begin by taking time to talk to each other and to family members and to discuss feelings and concerns calmly. They should also talk with a friend or another adult family member who is open-minded, caring, and willing to listen.

Step 2: Make a return visit to the doctor who provided the diagnosis to ask questions. Request names of specialists who provide the therapies recommended for the child. Dodd recommends having this follow-up visit no later than two weeks after the diagnosis. Parents should also ask about contact information for local autism associations. They can provide more information and access to other families for emotional and practical support.

Step 3: Read about ASD in general and about the particular diagnosis the child received. For example, what type of disorder is it and how will it affect all aspects of the child's life? When parents learn about ASD, they can begin to understand their child better. They can work out what the individual's needs and strengths are. Informed parents are better prepared to make decisions about services for the child or teen.

Numerous sources of information about ASD, such as books and articles, are available. Local autism associations can provide information and ideas on how to work with children and teens with

ASD. Parents and family members can also search the Internet as a starting point to learn more about ASD and available therapies. Dodd recommends discussing any findings with a trusted therapist or doctor before acting on them.

Step 4: Contact the services close to home that provide speech therapy, occupational therapy, and other necessary services. Parents should also contact centers that provide physical education classes, swimming lessons, and music and art therapy. Dodd encourages parents to talk to specialists to develop a structured daily schedule of classes and activities. These should provide stability in the child's world as well as teaching the child with ASD how to improve skills and build on strengths.

Step 5: Once the child has a therapy schedule, discuss with the specialist the possibility of enrolling the child in a local school. Many doctors believe that interacting with other mainstream children may help individuals with ASD improve their social and communication skills. Dodd recommends that, when possible, a child with ASD should attend school for at least one or two days per week. Schools should provide one-on-one class assistance when necessary. They should be able to help with the individual's needs, such as providing a quiet room if the child is upset by loud noises.

Step 6: Once parents have found caring therapists and have come up with a schedule that works for their child, they should stick with the schedule. They should also frequently check the individual's behavior for setbacks and improvements and change the plan as necessary.

COPING WITH EVERYDAY LIFE

Parents and families of children and teens with ASD face the challenge of learning to handle difficult situations every day. These include temper tantrums, aggression, and inappropriate repetitive behaviors

Alexa *(right)* is a two-year-old with autism. While the rest of her family gets ready for dinner, she wanders off to play with a garden hose. Repetitive and obsessive behaviors are common in autistic people and can be difficult for families to overcome.

and activities. Specialists, support groups, and other parents and siblings of ASD children can provide ideas for how to deal with these situations. In general, a consistent, firm, and calm strategy brings more positive outcomes than an upsetting, inconsistent approach.

STRATEGIES FOR OBSESSIVE BEHAVIORS

Obsessive repetitive habits interfere with the activities of the rest of the family. They also prevent the individual with ASD from moving forward to positive activities. Therapists have various strategies for limiting obsessive behaviors. In one case, an ASD child named Kate held a large photographic negative in her hand all the time. This habit attracted attention in public and prevented Kate from using her hand for other activities. Kate screamed loud and long every time the negative was torn or bent. She did not stop screaming until her parents gave her a new negative. This reaction occurred at home or in public, so her parents decided to eliminate the obsession using a system of gradual reduction.

Her parents made the negatives a tiny bit smaller every time they gave Kate a new one. Smaller negatives did not bother or upset Kate, until they were about one-half inch (1 centimeter) square. At this point, Kate developed a new behavior pattern. She held the small square negative in the center of her right palm with her middle finger. As soon as it got wet with sweat, which occurred often, Kate had a temper tantrum. But she still would not give up the negative. At this point, her parents decided not to give her any more pieces of negatives and to ignore her screams. After two difficult days, Kate lost the last piece of negative and soon forgot about it.

When objects cannot be cut down into smaller pieces, experts recommend reducing the time the child can have an object. For example, Cecilia wanted to carry a large dustpan and brush with her at all times. When her parents insisted that she leave them at home when going out, she protested with a tantrum. For a few days, her parents ignored her tantrums. They reassured her that she could have the dustpan and the brush when she returned home. In time, Cecilia accepted the new routine. She put the dustpan and brush in one particular place and said, "All ready for come back," when she went out.

DAILY CHALLENGES

Individuals with Asperger's syndrome who have well-developed language and other skills face different types of challenges. Many children and teens with Asperger's syndrome often want to be as independent as their non-ASD peers. They may be unwilling to accept parental or teacher authority and try to test the boundaries of that authority.

One way to cope with this behavior is to create environments that are structured and organized with fair rules. Rules should be provided in ways that are absolutely clear for the child or teen. Experts indicate that the best parents and teachers remain calm, firm, and consistent when insisting on following the rules. This strategy helps the individuals to develop personal rules for living over time.

Many individuals with Asperger's syndrome appear rude when they do not express respect for their parents or teachers. They do so because they often are unable to understand other people's thoughts and feelings.

Jordan is a thirteen-year-old boy with Asperger's syndrome. At school he has the habit of loudly interrupting the teacher's class when he wants to make a comment. He has been told many times that interrupting in this way is not appropriate. The rule is to raise his hand and wait for the teacher to call his name before speaking. The teacher knows that confrontation leads nowhere, so she tries to calmly and firmly negotiate with Jordan. She makes a deal with him. If he interrupts fewer than three times every class, the whole class will get pizza—Jordan's favorite food—for lunch one day that week.

By the ninth week of school, Jordan's class had not had pizza for lunch yet. But his classmates kept reminding him that they'll get the reward if he keeps quiet long enough. Eventually, the class and Jordan all enjoyed a pizza lunch together.

When one obsession or inappropriate habit disappears in a child with ASD, another one often comes along to take its place. However, it is also common that once the individual overcomes an unwanted routine, the replacement behaviors are less severe.

In practice, most parents find that give-and-take works well. The habits that comfort the child and do not cause stress, anxiety, or other difficulties can be left alone. For example, parents and siblings can support a child or teen with ASD if he or she likes to carry a small object in a pocket. As long as the child or the teen does not have a tantrum if the object is lost, the behavior is just fine. But it is highly recommended to try to change routines and behaviors that are harmful

www.usatoday.com

News
SECTION A

April 25, 2008

From the Pages of USA TODAY

Autism in the family brings kids together

It's very scary. Cause unknown. No known cure. Autism is like polio was when I was a kid. April is "Autism Awareness Month." Some alarmists are peddling the myth that autism can be caused by vaccinating children for various contagious diseases. That's nonsense, as reputable medical authorities agree. Autism is an inherited neurological disorder, but no one has figured out exactly what causes it or how to prevent it.

Our family has an autistic 8-year-old. Ali is one of our six chosen children all adopted at birth. My wife, Rachel, detected Ali's problem early. It was diagnosed as a very serious case of autism when he was age 2. Now, his case is mild to moderate. Things that have contributed to that marked improvement:

- Early and continuing professional help, carefully and constantly monitored by his mother.
- His five siblings. Alexis, 17; Karina, 11; Andre and Ariana, 10; his twin sister Rafi, 8. They enthusiastically have shared with him and taught him all normal childhood activities.

Ali's early tendency to be a loner has subsided strikingly. He loves being with his brother and sisters. They're involved with him in everything physical and mental. Bicycling to soccer. Computers to Wi-Fi. Even help with some school homework. Andre, who shares a room with him, told me this week: "Wow! Ali really is getting smart. I taught him how to play his Nintendo DS and now he's better at it than I am!"

How close Ali grows into a normal adult likely will be due largely to his siblings. He also is helping them understand and count their blessings.

—Al Neuharth

to the child or the family. Some harmful habits include destroying objects in the house, taking merchandise from stores without paying, smearing feces on the walls, ripping pages out of books, or tearing wallpaper. The goal is to find a balance between being too strict on the one hand and offering too little structure on the other. Each family is different, but staying calm, patient, creative, consistent, and having a good dose of humor are key elements for success. Success can be minor or major and often or seldom—it is different every day for each individual with ASD and his or her family.

DEALING WITH NEGATIVE CRITICISM

Relatives often provide help and support. They may listen to the parents and siblings of the child with ASD and provide relief and comfort. Other relatives and friends may have a less positive attitude.

They may think that a child with a disability is bad for the rest of the family. They forget that all families face challenges. They may try to blame one parent or the other or blame their ethnic heritage. They may reject the child with ASD and avoid seeing the family or inviting them to family reunions. They may think that all the problems are the parents' fault for using the wrong methods to deal with the child's inappropriate behavior. Other relatives may insist that there is nothing wrong with the child.

Experts advise that the best way to deal with negative criticism is to keep cool and calm. Parents and siblings of a child or a teen with ASD should provide information about the child but refuse to engage in arguments. If, in spite of these actions, a person's negative attitude does not change, experts recommend visiting these family members as little as possible.

CONCERNS ABOUT THE FUTURE

One of the main concerns parents express is the future of their ASD child in the event that, because of illness, injury, age, or death, they could no longer care for their child. Experts advise that parents arrange for the child to have a home and that they prepare wills or trusts to provide monetary support for future needs. If the individual with ASD has siblings, parents should talk to them to decide how the siblings will help one another to care for the brother or sister with ASD. Experts also recommend planning ahead to ensure that the ASD individual's service providers will be able to continue special education and therapy sessions.

"ME TIME" FOR PARENTS

Living with and caring for an individual with ASD can be hard work. ASD behaviors can be very challenging for families. For this reason, experts strongly recommend "me time"—taking a break—for parents. Me time lessens stress and helps family members stay patient, calm, and consistent.

Some family members, such as grandparents, uncles, or aunts, might be able to lend a hand. They might care for the individual with ASD while parents take time off to rest and relax. Members of support groups may also be able to help out when parents take time off.

BROTHERS AND SISTERS

Studies have shown that some siblings of individuals with ASD handle the situation well, while others have a much harder time and get stressed out. Siblings' coping abilities seem to depend on various factors. These factors include the severity of the disorder in their brother or sister, how disturbing the behavior is, the personalities of the siblings, and the attitude of the parents.

One of the most difficult issues for siblings of ASD children and teens is that their parents often have little time for them because they dedicate so much attention to the child with ASD. An effective strategy for families is for parents to schedule time to spend alone with their non-ASD children. Experts recommend one-on-one daily get-togethers, for example. This together time is a great way for parents to value and show love for the non-ASD siblings. Short daily meetings are more helpful than once in-a-while long meetings. One way to make time for the other children in the family is to arrange for help with chores so parents can have extra time.

Having a sibling with ASD who destroys toys, books, and other personal belongings can be hard to deal with. In this case, brothers and sisters need to have a safe place to lock their things and, if possible, their own room. The parents can also teach the ASD child not to touch or destroy objects. At the same time, parents are encouraged to do their best to replace the broken items and to reassure their non-ASD children that their rights will be respected. If the individual with ASD is aggressive toward siblings, parents and other caregivers should use therapy techniques to correct or limit this behavior.

For many families, ASD is a normal part of life. This family from Baltimore, Maryland, is like any other family in the United States—they face challenges, including one son's autism, and they get through them together.

www.usatoday.com

Life
SECTION D

July 24, 2008

From the Pages of USA TODAY

Flying can be a rough ride for autistic children, families

Letting airlines, kids know what to expect is key

With heightened security regulations and frequent delays, airplane travel can be an unpleasant ordeal for anyone. For a child who becomes anxious in close quarters, may have trouble communicating and is sensitive to loud noises, it can be terrifying.

Autism has been getting more attention in the past five years through advocacy groups such as Autism Speaks and the Autism Society of America. But it still gets negative attention: Last week, syndicated talk radio host Michael Savage said on his show that 99% of the time, a child with autism was just "a brat who hasn't been told to cut the act out." The comment drew protests from the advocacy groups.

His comments probably refer to the behavior autistic children can exhibit when they feel anxious, particularly in unfamiliar situations. They can have meltdowns that involve crying, screaming or kicking. Last month, Janice Farrell of Cary, N.C., and her 2-year-old autistic son, Jarret, were removed from their American Eagle flight after Jarret began crying and screaming uncontrollably. (The airline says Farrell also refused to stow her bag in the proper place, which she denies.)

Airline travel, which is a necessity for many families, has many characteristics

In spite of sometimes frustrating situations, many brothers and sisters enjoy playing with and teaching their siblings with ASD. Many times, they are more successful than their parents at some teaching techniques. However, placing too much responsibility on the shoulders of siblings can be overwhelming. Parents must make sure that the siblings have time to pursue their own interests.

One way parents can help their children understand ASD is by that can trigger such meltdowns. It breaks the normal routine—which many autistic children find stressful because they have trouble anticipating what will happen. Airplane travel involves sitting still for long periods and being surrounded by crowds, says Rebecca Landa, director of the Center for Autism at the Kennedy Krieger Institute in Baltimore [Maryland].

"Take all the issues (normal adults) have with flying, magnify that by 100, and put that into a child's body," Landa says. James Gillespie of Philadelphia [Pennsylvania], whose son has autism, says: "You will run into any number of well-intentioned people who just look at you as if you're a bad parent. There was a time that I was pretty defensive about it."

Both Landa and Kelly Ernsperger counsel families in the greater Indianapolis [Indiana] area who are coping with autism. They recommend preparing children in the days leading up to the trip by making sure they know exactly what to expect.

"I encourage families to go online and try to get pictures of the airport terminals and planes and destination," Ernsperger says. These pictures, along with conversations about what the child will be doing, help families create "social stories" so children are better able to anticipate exactly what will happen to them.

Landa also recommends letting the child make some choices—such as choosing his seat—to defray some of the anxiety. Creating simple rules to define the social situation also helps. Gillespie made such a rule for Brendan to let him know what topics were off-limits on airplanes: terrorists, crashing and dying.

He and other parents say snacks and earphones for a child's favorite music or movies are also a must. It's important to let the airlines know about the situation so they can accommodate the family as well. Many airlines have taken steps to make sure that flight attendants and airport employees are trained to assist customers with disabilities.

"It's best to think, 'How can I be helpful?'" Landa says, whether that is refraining from making a critical remark or offering to hold something for the family.
—*Rebecca Kaplan*

explaining what ASD is and how it affects their sibling's behavior. This usually helps siblings deal with some of the frustration, impatience, and rejection of the child with ASD. The explanations should be simple for young siblings. For older siblings, parents may choose to use books, brochures, and videos as teaching tools.

Teens with an ASD sibling may also benefit from talking with other people living in a similar situation. It's not easy being the brother or sister of an individual with ASD. Exchanging ideas and feelings about living with a child in the autistic spectrum may help teens develop more patience with their sibling. Teens also find it helpful to get help developing a positive attitude, to take things one day at a time with a sense of humor, to use lots of patience and understanding, to take me time, and to rely on parental support.

TONY'S STORY

Tony is an adult with Asperger's syndrome. His young son, Ted, has also been diagnosed with Asperger. Tony wishes that his parents had told him about his diagnosis when he was younger. If they had, he wouldn't have been left to wonder why he felt so different from other kids. When Ted was about seven, Tony decided to tell his son about his disorder. He found a book that helped explain it. Tony and Ted looked at the book together and talked about the syndrome. Afterward, Tony said, Ted seemed okay with his diagnosis. Tony was glad he told him.

HELPING INDIVIDUALS COPE

How do parents tell their child that he or she has ASD? Should they tell the child? Informing a child of his diagnosis is a parent's decision. If the child is too young, he or she might not be able to understand the diagnosis. However, as children grow up, they become more self aware. Experts recommend that parents sit with the child and inform him or her of the diagnosis and explain the family's plan to help.

Individuals react differently when they learn of their ASD. Those with the most severe forms of the disorder might be too disabled to understand their condition. On the other hand, many children and teens with Asperger's syndrome respond to the news by challenging themselves positively and working very hard to learn coping skills. Other children in the spectrum respond to the news by being more patient with themselves to avoid frustrations at school or at home.

Some individuals with Asperger's syndrome may have a difficult time handling their feelings. They may be more anxious than others on the spectrum about fitting in and "being normal." This can lead to depression, anxiety, stress, and temper outbursts. A recent study reported that 85 percent of children with Asperger's syndrome show depression and anxiety, as compared to 15 percent of the general population.

Symptoms of depression include disorganization, lack of focus and attention, isolation, fatigue, crying bouts, or talk of suicide. Asperger individuals should be encouraged to talk honestly about their feelings. And if anyone talks about committing suicide, he or she should get immediate professional help.

To help teens cope, experts recommend that parents and teachers offer a high level of consistency as well as ways to cope with stressful situations. Strategies that are presented in a way the individual can understand are most effective.

Experts recommend that parents, teachers, specialists, and other people involved remain calm, predictable, and clear in their interactions with ASD teens. Avoid sarcasm and certain kinds of jokes, as people with ASD tend to interpret things literally.

CHAPTER SEVEN

THE JOURNEY AHEAD

ANTONIO'S STORY

To cut down on his mom's daily commute, Antonio and his family moved from one Chicago, Illinois, suburb to another. It is only a distance of about 20 miles (32 km), but Antonio had to work hard to adjust. Like many people with ASD, he finds changes in routine very stressful. Antonio misses friends and teachers from his old school, and he is anxious about having to meet all new people when he starts his new school in August. But he is very excited about one aspect of the move. The family's new house has a big, fenced-in backyard—perfect for the golden retriever they just adopted. Antonio loves dogs. He has ever since his mom first took him to canine-assisted therapy when he was four.

Antonio's mom, Tina, had read that dogs can help ASD children come out of their shells. Playing with the animals helps the children focus on their environment. The first time Tina saw Antonio laughing and petting his therapy dog, she knew the therapy would do her son good. His interest in and affection for animals has continued into his teen years.

And Tina continues to search for therapies to help Antonio. She slowly makes the new therapies part of his life. She also looks for role models—professionals, family members, and friends who might help Antonio in the adult world.

We have come a long way since Kanner and Asperger in understanding ASD. For many years, people thought that children developed ASD because their parents did not show affection and did not care for them. More recently, we've come to know that the autism spectrum is a range of developmental disorders caused by genetic and environmental factors. Some of the next questions to answer are, Which are the specific genes involved in ASD? And how do the interactions between the genes and the environment disrupt brain development to produce a different kind of mind? Research is in progress to answer these questions.

Modern researchers know that the children Kanner and Asperger described represent two of the many forms or expressions of ASD. The ways autistic behaviors can be expressed are as varied as the individuals living with ASD. There is no single form of autism.

Individuals in the spectrum may also face other challenges. They may have difficulties perceiving the environment with their senses, coordinating body movements, or sleeping. They may also have trouble understanding what other people think or feel. They may be intellectually delayed. They may have difficulty planning their daily activities and getting organized. At the same time, a few people with the disorder—the savants—have mathematical, musical, or artistic abilities way beyond what most people have.

Although there is no cure for ASD, therapies are available to help people in the autistic spectrum develop skills and lead more productive lives. Parents have played a very important role in raising public awareness about ASD. The journey ahead for scientists, doctors, therapists, parents, and individuals with ASD is no less exciting and challenging than the journey in the past several decades.

FURTHER RESEARCH

The list is long for areas in need of further research. For example, professionals need new tools to diagnose the disorder earlier. Many experts believe that the sooner a diagnosis is made and therapies begin, the higher the chance the major symptoms will lessen in severity. Much research is under way to try to find early biological clues. For example, knowing specific genes involved in ASD could be used to provide an early diagnosis, perhaps even before the child is born.

Researchers are also working to better understand the science of attention, sleep, physical coordination, and speech. Research is in progress to try to make clear why individuals with ASD have difficulties planning, thinking, and understanding other people's thoughts and feelings. A direct link between the immune system and ASD has yet to be found, but researchers continue to explore the possibility of a link.

More research is also needed to explain why setbacks occur in individuals who are apparently making progress under therapy. Part of that research involves a better understanding of the brain abnormalities associated with ASD.

Many therapies are currently available for individuals with ASD, but little is known about how effective most of them are.

This child is one of a growing number of Somali American children in Minnesota who have autism. More research is needed to determine why the rate is unusually high.

Measuring effectiveness is not easy. How well a particular therapy works does not depend on the therapy alone. It also depends on the particular characteristics of the ASD individual, as well as on the therapist. One particular therapy might work for one individual, but not for another.

AWARENESS ABOUT THE DISORDER

The history of ASD shows that when more people were made aware of the disorder, research increased, therapies developed, and governments increased their support for services. Parents have created active groups that have played an essential role in developing increased awareness. One way to develop public awareness has been to organize community events, such as public talks and marathons. During these gatherings, people learn about ASD and meet affected individuals and their families. Some highly functioning individuals with ASD, such as Temple Grandin, as well as parents, scientists, and doctors have written books about their personal experiences and have given talks about the syndrome.

ASD support groups exist all over the world. In the United States, the ASA, Autism Speaks, and the Cure Autism Now (CAN) Foundation are just a few among many. In the United Kingdom, the National Autistic Society (NAS) is the leading organization for people with autism and those who care for them. In Canada the Autism Society of Canada and similar regional groups have played a major role in creating awareness about ASD.

SERVICES

Experts agree that ASD requires lifelong therapy and support. Yet many individuals do not receive appropriate services. Many young

www.usatoday.com

USA TODAY

News
SECTION A

August 19, 2009

From the Pages of USA TODAY

Kids with autism deserve better

Today, millions of children with special needs such as autism disorders are not getting the therapy they need or the education they deserve. Their parents are powerless to help them.

Marc Thiessen's son is a 5-year-old with Asperger's syndrome. Each year has been a battle with insurers to cover the speech and occupational therapy he needs. His parents also battled with the school district that was constantly trying to cut back his services.

When it came time for him to move to kindergarten, it turned out that the Alexandria, Va., public schools system did not have an Asperger's program. Instead, the school district proposed putting him in a regular kindergarten classroom with more than 20 kids and reduced services. Rather than put him in a situation in which he was sure to fail, his parents found a private school in Maryland—a three-hour daily commute.

Only 11 states require private insurance plans to cover the types of therapy that have received the endorsement of the American Academy of Pediatrics and National Academy of Sciences. And school districts, increasingly strapped for funds, often fail to provide the individual attention needed for children with autism and other challenges.

This needs to change.

—*Marc Thiessen and Michael O'Hanlon*

children receive therapy, but only limited support and services are currently available for teens and adults.

Effective education for teens and adults with ASD should include sex education and strategies to make the change from high school to further education easier. ASD teens and adults also need help to learn how to live independently and how to socialize in the workplace.

In the United States, as part of the Children's Health Act of 2000, Congress has requested that scientists work with one another in their research about ASD. A project called the Studies to Advance Autism Research and Treatment (STAART) Network has been created to help scientists collaborate. The project brings together eight excellent research centers across the country in a five-year program. The centers carry out research into causes, diagnosis, early detection, and treatment of ASD. Scientists share the results of these investigations with ASD groups as well as with the general public via Internet sites.

Autistic spectrum disorders occur across the globe. No geographical or social barriers limit ASD. Individuals with ASD live in the most inaccessible villages in Asia and in the richest suburbs in the United States. All over the world, scientists, doctors, parents, and individuals with ASD work every day to try to better understand ASD. They exchange the information they have gathered in national and international meetings. The journey to fully understand and hopefully one day cure ASD is under way.

GLOSSARY

amygdala: an almond-shaped area of gray brain matter associated with fear, aggression, visual learning, and memory

antisocial: behavior characterized by aggression or violence toward others

Asperger's syndrome: a pervasive developmental disorder characterized by mild to severe problems in speech, socialization, and behavior

autism: a pervasive developmental disorder that can be characterized by severe problems in speech, socialization, and behavior

autism spectrum disorders (ASD): a group of pervasive developmental disorders comprising autism, Asperger's syndrome, and pervasive developmental disorder–not otherwise specified (PDD-NOS)

central nervous system: the portion of the nervous system that includes the brain and the spinal cord

chelation therapy: medical treatment that involves administering a chemical that binds to and eliminates metals such as lead, mercury, calcium, or cadmium from the body

childhood disintegrative disorder (CDD): a disorder in which a child shows a period of normal development followed by a loss of language, social, cognitive, or motor skills

cognitive: relating to conscious thought and reasoning

comorbidity factor: other diseases present at the same time as the disease in question

corpus callosum: the network of nerve fibers linking the left and right sides of the brain

cortex: the outer layer of the brain

depression: an illness characterized by persistent feelings of sadness and hopelessness

developmental disorder: an impairment that affects the brain and interferes with the normal development of the mind

echolalia: the repetition of words spoken by others

electroencephalogram (EEG): a measurement and record of the electrical activity of a brain

empathy: ability to identify with and understand another person's feelings and difficulties

environmental: outside factors that may affect a person's development or health

epilepsy: a medical disorder of the brain characterized by periodic convulsions and sometimes loss of consciousness

functional magnetic resonance imaging (fMRI): a medical test that measures changes in the blood flow within the brain

hemispheres: the two sides of the brain

impairment: the lessening or absence of a particular physical or mental function

incidence: the number of new cases of a defined disorder occurring in a population over a period of time

macrocephaly: a condition marked by an unusually large head

microcephaly: a condition marked by an unusually small head

neuroimaging: techniques that provide two- or three-dimensional pictures of brain activity

neurologist: a medical doctor who specializes in the nervous system and disorders that affect it

neuron: the cell that is the basic functional unit of the nervous system

neurotransmitters: chemicals that help regulate brain activity

obsessive: recurrent and persistent

obsessive-compulsive disorder: a disorder characterized by a tendency to have excessive unwanted thoughts or to perform repetitive rituals

pervasive: having the quality to permeate or be present throughout

pervasive developmental disorder: a group of disorders that affect an individual's development in several areas, such as speech and social skills

pervasive developmental disorder–not otherwise specified (PDD-NOS): one of the three categories of autism spectrum disorders; also called atypical autism

placebo: an inactive substance used as a control in an experiment to test the effectiveness of a medicinal drug

positron-emission tomography (PET): a medical test that measures the amount of glucose and oxygen used by brain cells for energy

prevalence: the proportion of individuals in a population who have a defined disorder at a given point in time

prognosis: a prediction of the probable course and outcome of a disease or disorder

psychosis: a severe mental disorder characterized by delusions, hallucination, and distorted perceptions of reality. Schizophrenia is a type of psychosis.

receptor: a structure on the surface of a cell that binds to a specific molecule and mediates the transmission of a message to the interior of the cell

Rett syndrome: a complex disorder of the nervous system characterized by the loss of the ability to move the hands with a purpose

savant: a person who is exceptionally gifted in a specialized area while performing in the average or below-average range in all other areas

schizophrenia: a severe psychiatric disorder characterized by emotional instability, detachment from reality, hallucinations, and withdrawal into the self

selective serotonin reuptake inhibitors (SSRIs): a group of antidepressants that work by increasing the amount of serotonin available to the nerve cells in the brain

sensory perception: detection of environmental stimuli using the senses

spectrum: a broad range of related qualities

stereotyped behavior: a persistent, inflexible pattern of behavior

synapse: a junction between two nerve cells, where one end of a nerve fiber almost touches another cell in order to transmit signals

syndrome: a group of symptoms that taken together characterize a disease, a disorder, or another atypical condition

theory of central coherence: the view that ASD individuals have a fragmented focus that results in trouble integrating, or putting together, pieces of information into a whole

theory of mind: a concept that describes a person's awareness that other people have beliefs and desires different from his or her own

triad: a group of three

RESOURCES

Autism Society of America (ASA)
4340 East-West Hwy, Suite 350 • Bethesda, MD 20814
800-3AUTISM (800-328-8476), 301-657-0881
http://www.autism-society.org

Founded in 1965 by doctors Bernard Rimland and Ruth Sullivan and by other parents of children with autism, ASA is a grassroots autism organization. It provides information about autism treatment, education, research, and advocacy. The group works to increase public awareness of the daily issues facing people on the spectrum and works to ensure appropriate services for individuals of all ages.

Autism Society of Canada
Box 22017, 1670 Heron Road • Ottawa, Ontario K1V 0C2
866-476-8440, 613-789-8943
http://www.autismsocietycanada.ca

Founded in 1976, the Autism Society of Canada is a national charitable organization. It provides information on understanding ASD, current research programs, and treatment and education strategies. Through regional offices and programs, it also provides support and information for people with ASD and their families.

Autism Speaks
1 East 33rd Street, 4th Floor • New York, NY 10016
212-252-8584
http://www.autismspeaks.org

Autism Speaks is a charitable organization with the mission of education, awareness, and fund-raising. The organization works to increase public awareness of autism spectrum disorders, funds research into the causes of and treatments for autism, and advocates for the needs of individuals with autism and their families. Student Clubs for Autism Speaks (SCAS) furthers this mission by involving middle school, high school, and college students in campaigns and fund-raising.

Doug Flutie Jr. Foundation for Autism, Inc.
PO Box 767 • Framingham, MA 01702
866-3AUTISM (866-328-8476), 508-270-8855
http://www.dougflutiejrfoundation.org

In the early 1990s, National Football League quarterback Doug Flutie and his wife, Laurie, learned that their three-year-old son, Doug Jr., had autism. The Fluties began raising funds for autism awareness, and in 2000, they established the Doug Flutie Jr. Foundation for Autism, Inc. The foundation's goals include education and public awareness. The foundation also raises funds for family support and provides recreational opportunities to improve the quality of life for individuals with autism.

National Autism Association
1330 W. Schatz Lane • Nixa, MO 65714
877-622-2884
http://www.nationalautismassociation.org

The National Autism Association bases its mission on the idea that autism is a treatable disorder. The association works to fund research, education, and advocacy. It also works to raise public and professional awareness of possible environmental factors in neurological damage.

The National Autistic Society (NAS)
393 City Road • London EC1V 1NG • United Kingdom
+44 (0)20 7833 2299
http://www.autism.org.uk

The United Kingdom's National Autistic Society campaigns for education and social services for people with autism. The staff trains volunteers and organizes conferences and workshops. The society's website provides information about autism in several languages, news, and local events in Great Britain.

TACA (Talk About Curing Autism)
370 Bristol Street, Suite 340 • Costa Mesa, CA 92626
949-640-4401
http://www.tacanow.com

Talk About Curing Autism (TACA) provides information, resources, and support to families affected by autism. For families who have just received the autism diagnosis, TACA aims to speed up the cycle time from the autism diagnosis to effective treatments. TACA helps to strengthen the autism community by connecting families and the professionals who can help them, allowing them to share stories and information to help people with autism be the best they can be.

SOURCE NOTES

26 Leo Kanner, "Autistic Disturbances of Affective Contact," *Nervous Child*, 1943, 242.

27 Ibid., 245.

27 Ibid.

SELECTED BIBLIOGRAPHY

American Academy of Pediatrics. "AAP Issues Guidelines on Diagnosing and Management of Autism." AAP. May 7, 2001. http://www.aap.org/advocacy/archives/mayautism.htm.

American Psychiatric Association. *Diagnostic and Statistical Manual of Mental Disorders*. 4th ed. American Psychiatric Association: Washington, DC, 2000.

Arking, D. E., et. al. "A Common Genetic Variant in the Neurexin Superfamily Member CNTNAP2 Increases Familial Risk of Autism," *American Journal of Human Genetics* 82, no 1 (January 2008): 150–159.

Artigas-Pallarés, J. "Autismo y Vacunas: ¿Punto Final?" *Revista de Neurología* 50 (2010): S91–S99.

Ashwood, Paul, and J. Van de Water. "A Review of Autism and the Immune Response." *Clinical and Developmental Immunology* 11, no. 2 (June 2004): 165–174.

Asperger, H., *Die Autistichen Psychopathen im Kindesalter, Archiv fur Psychiatrie und Nervenkrankheiten* 117 (1944): 76–136. Translated by Uta Frith as "'Autistic Psychopathy in Childhood." *Autism and Asperger Syndrome* 37–92. Cambridge: Cambridge University Press, 1991.

Atladóttir, Hjördís Ó., Marianne G. Pedersen, Poul Thorsen, Preben Bo Mortensen, Bent Deleuran, William W. Eaton, and Erik T. Parner. "Association of Family History of Autoimmune Diseases and Autism Spectrum Disorders." *Pediatrics* 124, no. 2 (August 2009): 687–694.

Bashe, Patricia Romanowski, and B. L. Kirby. *The Oasis Guide to Asperger Syndrome: Advice, Support, Insight, and Inspiration*. 2nd ed. New York: Crown Publishers, 2005.

Bauman, Margaret, and Thomas L. Kemper, eds. *The Neurobiology of Autism*. Baltimore: Johns Hopkins University Press, 2005.

Biklen, Douglas. *Autism and the Myth of the Person Alone*. New York: New York University Press, 2005.

Bradstreet, James Jeffrey, Scott Smith, Matthew Baral, and Daniel A. Rossignol. "Biomarker-Guided Interventions of Clinically Relevant Conditions Associated with Autism Spectrum Disorders and Attention Deficit Hyperactive Disorder," *Alterative Medicine Review* 15, no. 1 (2010): 15–32.

Casanova, Manuel F., ed. *Recent Developments in Autism Research.* New York: Nova Scientific Books, 2005.

Coleman, Mary, ed. *The Neurology of Autism.* New York: Oxford University Press, 2005.

DiCicco-Bloom, Emanuel, Catherine Lord, Lonnie Zwaigenbaum, Eric Courchesne, Stephen R. Dager, Christop Schmitz, Robert T. Schultz, Jacqueline Crawley, and Larry J. Young. "The Developmental Neurobiology of Autism Spectrum Disorder." *Journal of Neuroscience*, no. 26 (June 28, 2006): 6,897–6,906.

Fombonne, Eric. "The Prevalence of Autism." *Journal of the American Medical Association* 289, no. 1 (January 1, 2003): 87–89.

Frith, Uta. *Autism and Asperger Syndrome.* Cambridge: Cambridge University Press, 1991.

Frith, Uta, and Elisabeth Hill, eds. *Autism: Mind and Brain.* New York: Oxford University Press, 2003.

Grether, Judith, Meredith C. Anderson, Lisa A. Croen, Daniel Smith and Gayle C. Windham. "Risk of Autism and Increasing Maternal and Paternal Age in a Large North American Population," *American Journal of Epidemiology* 170, no. 9 (November 2009): 1,118–1,126.

Kanner, Leo. "Autistic Disturbances of Affective Contact." *Nervous Child,* 1943, 217–250.

——. "Follow-Up Study of Eleven Autistic Children Originally Reported in 1943." *Journal of Autism and Childhood Schizophrenia,* April–June 1971, 119–145.

King, M., and Peter Bearman, "Diagnostic Change and the Increased Prevalence of Autism." *International Journal of Epidemiology* 38, no. 5 (October 2009): 1,224–1,234.

Kogan, Michael D., Stephen J. Blumberg, Laura A. Schieve, Coleen A. Boyle, James M. Perrin, Reem M. Ghandour, Gopal K. Singh, Bonnie B. Strickland, Edwin Trevathan, and Peter C. van Dyck. "Prevalence of Parent-Reported Diagnosis of Autism Spectrum Disorder Among Children in the US, 2007" *Pediatrics* 124, no. 5 (November 2009): 1,395–1,403.

Lawton, Graham. "The Autism Epidemic That Never Was." *New Scientist*, August 13, 2005, 37–40.

Mathews, T. J. and B. E. Hamilton. "Delayed Childbearing: More Women Are Having Their First Child Later in Life." Centers for Disease Control and Prevention. August 2009. http://www.cdc.gov/nchs/data/databriefs/db21.htm (October 13, 2010).

Mayes, Linda C., and Donald J. Cohen. *The Yale Child Study Center Guide to Understanding Your Child: Healthy Development from Birth to Adolescence*. New Haven, CT: Yale University Press, 2002.

Morrow, Eric M. et.al. "Identifying Autism Loci and Genes by Tracing Recent Shared Ancestry," *Science* 321, no. 5,886 (July 2008): 218–223.

Pratter, C. D., and R. Zylstra. "Autism: A Medical Primer." *American Family Physician*, November 1, 2002, 1,667–1,675.

Reichenberg, Abraham, Raz Gross, Sven Sandin, and Ezra S. Susser. "Advancing Paternal and Maternal Age Are Both Important for Autism Risk," *American Journal of Public Health* 100, no. 5 (May 2010): 772–773.

Schneider, Wolfgang, R. Schumann-Hengsteler, and B. Sodian. *Young Children's Cognitive Development, Interrelationships among Executive Functioning, Working Memory, Verbal Ability, and Theory of Mind*. Mahwah, NJ: Lawrence Erlbaum, 2005.

Schreibman, Laura. *The Science and Fiction of Autism*. Cambridge, MA: Harvard University Press, 2005.

Sicile-Kira, Chantal. *Autism Spectrum Disorders: The Complete Guide to Understanding Autism, Asperger's Syndrome, Pervasive Developmental Disorders, and Other ASD*. New York: Berkeley Publishing, 2004.

Treffert, Darold A., and D. Christensen. "Inside the Mind of a Savant." *Scientific American*, December 2005, 108–113.

Volkmar, Fred R., R. Paul, A. Klin, and D. Cohen. *Handbook of Autism and Pervasive Developmental Disorders*. 3rd ed. Vol.1, *Diagnosis, Development, Neurology, and Behavior*. Hoboken, NJ: John Wiley, 2005.

Wing, Lorna. "Asperger's Syndrome: A Clinical Account." *Psychological Medicine* 11 (1981): 115–129.

———. "The Epidemiology of Autistic Spectrum Disorders: Is the Prevalence Rising?" *Mental Retardation and Developmental Disabilities Research Reviews* 8 (2002): 151–161.

———. "The History of Ideas on Autism." *Autism: The International Journal of Research and Practice* 1 (1997):13–24.

———. "The Spectrum of Autistic Disorders" *Hospital Practice* 65, no. 9 (2004): 542–545.

Wing, Lorna, and J. Gold. "Severe Impairments of Social Interaction and Associated Abnormalities in Children: Epidemiology and Classification." *Journal of Autism and Developmental Disorders* 9, no.1 (1979): 11–29.

FURTHER READING AND WEBSITES

For Students

Brynie, Faith Hickman. *101 Questions Your Brain Has Asked about Itself*. Minneapolis: Twenty-First Century Books, 2008.

Dickinson, John. "Myths about Savants." *New Scientist*, July 30, 2005.

Dowshen, Steven. "Controversial Study Withdrawn Suggesting Link between Autism and MMR Vaccine." *KidsHealth*, March 2004.

Frith, Uta. "Autism." *Scientific American*, June 1993.

Grandin, Temple, and K. Duffy. *Developing Talents: Careers for Individuals with Asperger Syndrome and High-Functioning Autism*. Shawnee Mission, KS: Autism Asperger Publishing Company, 2004.

Grandin, Temple, and Margaret M. Scariano. *Emergence: Labeled Autistic*. New York: Warner Books, 1996. First published 1986 by Arena Press.

Greenfeld, Karl Taro. "The Homecoming." *Sports Illustrated*, October 10, 2005.

Jolliffe, Therese, R. Lansdown, and C. Robinson. "Autism: A Personal Account." *Communication* 26, no. 3 (1992).

Living in the Spectrum. Vol. 1, *Autism and Asperger's*. Royal Oak, MI: Mindscape Productions, 2004. CD-ROM.

Mukerjee, M. "A Transparent Enigma." *Scientific American*, June 2004.

Mukhopadhyay, Tito Rajarshi. *The Mind Tree, a Miraculous Child Breaks the Silence of Autism*. New York: Arcade, 2003.

Peek, Fran. *The Real Rain Man*. Salt Lake City: Harkness Publishing, 1996.

Rosenberg, Marsha Sarah. *Coping When a Brother or Sister Is Autistic*. New York: Rosen, 2001.

Tammet, Daniel. *Born on a Blue Day: Inside the Extraordinary Mind of an Autistic Savant*; a Memoir. New York: Free Press, 2007.

——. *Embracing the Wide Sky: A Tour Across the Horizons of the Mind*. New York: Free Press, 2009.

TeensHealth. "Autism." Nemours Foundation. April 2008. http:// www.kidshealth. org/teen/school_jobs/school/autism.html (May 28, 2008).

Treffert, Darold A. "Gilles Tréhin: The City of Urville." Wisconsin Medical Society. 2008. http://www.wisconsinmedicalsociety.org/ savant_syndrome/savant_profiles/ gilles_trehin (May 28, 2008).

——. "Kim Peek, the Real Rainman." Wisconsin Medical Society, December 21,2009. http://www.wisconsinmedicalsociety.org/savant_syndrome/savant_profiles/kim_ peek#updates (October 13, 2010).

Willey, Liane Holliday. *Pretending to Be Normal: Living with Asperger's Syndrome*. London: Jessica Kingsley, 1999.

——, ed. *Asperger Syndrome in Adolescence: Living the Ups, the Downs, and Things in Between*. London: Jessica Kingsley, 2003.

For Parents and Teachers
Abrams, Philip, and L. Henriques. *The Autism Spectrum Parents' Daily Helper*. Berkeley, CA: Ulysses Press, 2004.

Attwood, Tony. *Asperger's Syndrome: A Guide for Parents and Professionals*. London: Jessica Kingsley, 1998.

Cutler, Eustacia. *A Thorn in My Pocket: Temple Grandin's Mother Tells a Family Story*. Arlington, TX: Future Horizons, 2004.

Dodd, Susan. *Understanding Autism*. Marrickville: Elsevier Australia, 2005.

Eliot, Lise. *What's Going on in There? How the Brain and Mind Develop in the First Five Years of Life*. New York: Bantam Books, 2000.

Exkorn, Karen Siff. *The Autism Sourcebook: Everything You Need to Know about Diagnosis, Treatment, Coping, and Healing*. New York: Regan Books, 2005.

Frith, Uta. *Autism, Explaining the Enigma*. 2nd ed. Oxford, UK: Blackwell Publishing, 2003.

Grandin, Temple. *Thinking in Pictures: and Other Reports of My Life with Autism.* 2nd ed. New York: Vintage Books, 2006.

———. *The Way I See It*, 2nd ed. Arlington, TX: Future Horizons, 2011.

Happe, Francesca, and Uta Frith, ed. *Autism and Talent.* Oxford: Oxford University Press, USA, 2010.

Mont, Daniel. *A Different Kind of Boy: A Father's Memoir about Raising a Gifted Child with Autism.* London: Jessica Kingsley, 2002.

Myers, Martin, and Diego Pineda, *Do Vaccines Cause That? A Guide for Evaluating Vaccine Safety Concerns.* Galveston, TX:Immunizations for Public Health, 2008.

Nazeer, Kamran. *Send in the Idiots: Stories from the Other Side of Autism.* New York: Bloomsbury, 2006.

Sacks, Oliver. *An Anthropologist in Mars: Seven Paradoxical Tales.* New York: Alfred A. Knopf, 1995.

Treffert, Darold A. "The Savant Syndrome: Islands of Genius." Wisconsin Medical Society. 2008. http://www.wisconsinmedicalsociety .org/savant_syndrome/ (May 28, 2008).

Wallis, Claudia. "Inside the Autistic Mind." *Time*, May 15, 2006.

Williams, Donna. *Everyday Heaven: Journeys beyond the Stereotypes of Autism.* London: Jessica Kingsley, 2004.

Wing, Lorna. *The Autistic Spectrum: A Parents' Guide to Understanding and Helping Your Child.* Berkeley, CA: Ulysses Press, 2001.

Zager, Dianne. *Autism Spectrum Disorders, Identification, Education, and Treatment.* 3rd ed. Mahwah, NJ: Lawrence Erlbaum, 2005.

INDEX

ABOUT THE AUTHOR

Ana Maria Rodriguez was born in Buenos Aires, Argentina. She has a Ph.D. in biology and immunology from the Venezuelan Institute for Scientific Research. In 1987 she began her postdoctoral work at the University of Texas, Southwestern Medical Center, Dallas. Besides doing research in the fields of biology, microbiology, immunology, genetics, cell biology, and biochemistry, Rodriguez taught basic and advanced courses for graduate and undergraduate students. She has published more than twenty articles in science journals about her research. Rodriguez has also published more than eighty articles and fourteen books for young readers.

PHOTO ACKNOWLEDGMENTS

The images in this book are used with the permission of: © Living Art Enterprises/ Photo Researchers, Inc., pp. 1, 3; Evan Eile/USA TODAY, p. 7; © Silvia Morara/CORBIS, p. 8; © Lara Jo Regan/Getty Images, p. 13; © © Photograph by Greystone Studios. Image courtesy of the Alan Mason Chesney Medical Archives of the Johns Hopkins Medical Institutions, p. 25; © Marco Garcia/USA TODAY, p. 32; © Photo by Kathleen Turley/Tri-Valley Herald/ZUMA Press, p. 37; © Laura Westlund/Independent Picture Service, p. 45; © Annabella Bluesky/Photo Researchers, Inc., p. 53; © Jason LaVeris/ FilmMagic/Getty Images, p. 75; © Vincent Du/Rueters/CORBIS, p. 78; © Michael Macor/San Francisco Chronicle/CORBIS, p. 84; © Janine Wiedel/Photolibary/Alamy, p. 86; © Ali Jarekji/Reuters/CORBIS, p. 88; © Kate Karwan Burgess/ZUMA Press, p. 92; © Melissa Lyttle/St Petersburg Times/ZUMApress.com, p. 97; © ALGERINA PERNA/MCT /Landov, p. 103; © Jim Gehrz/Star Tribune/ZUMA Press, p. 110.

Front Cover: © Living Art Enterprises/Photo Researchers, Inc.